ALL WHO ARE
THIRSTY

ALL WHO ARE THIRSTY

DISCOVERING THE FULLNESS OF THE HOLY SPIRIT

Jennifer A. Miskov, Ph.D.
Carrie Judd Montgomery
Heidi Baker, Ph.D.

© Copyright 2022 Jennifer A. Miskov

Jennifer A. Miskov asserts the moral right to be identified as the author and editor of this work.

All rights reserved. No part of this publication may be reproduced, stored in a retrieval system, or transmitted in any form or by any means—for example, electronic, photocopy, recording—without the prior written permission of the author and publisher. The only exception is brief quotations in printed reviews.

Published by Silver to Gold

Anaheim, CA 92807 USA

www.silvertogold.com

ISBN: 0-9842370-3-8

ISBN-13: 978-0-9842370-3-6

Printed in the United States of America

Cover Design by David Stoddard. Learn more at MediaRevelation.com

Interior Design by Terry Clifton.

Photographs of Carrie Judd Montgomery used by permission of the Berry family and the Flower Pentecostal Heritage Center. I am grateful to the Flower Pentecostal Heritage Center for scanning *Triumphs of Faith* to make Carrie's works available in disc form and for granting permission to use Carrie's photograph. Carrie's writings are currently in the public domain.

Every effort has been made to get permissions for other copyrighted material to be used; however, if anything has been missed, please contact us and changes will be made in future printings.

All Scripture is taken from New International Version unless otherwise noted. Holy Bible, New International Version®, NIV® Copyright © 1973, 1978, 1984, 2011 by Biblica, Inc.® Used by permission. All rights reserved worldwide.

Other Scripture taken from New King James Version®. Copyright © 1982 by Thomas Nelson. Used by permission. All rights reserved.

Special thanks to my agent Steve Lawson for his support and encouragement in this work, Lauren Stinton for her incredible editing skills, and David Stoddard for his creativity in bringing the cover to life.

Visit the author's website at JenMiskov.com.

On the last day, that great day of the feast, Jesus stood and cried out, saying, "If anyone thirsts, let him come to Me and drink. He who believes in Me, as the Scripture has said, out of his heart will flow rivers of living water."

JOHN 7:37–38 (NKJV)

"HO, EVERY ONE THAT THIRSTETH!"

Isa. lv: 1.

HEARKEN, O my weary spirit,
  To the sweet words ringing clear,
There are waters in the desert
  And thou needst not faint and fear;
"Every one that thirsteth, come ye!"
  Hear that message as it falls,
O my soul, if thou art thirsting,
  Thou art then the one it calls.

Hearken still, my soul, and wonder,
  "He that hath no money buy,"
Hast thou not a price to offer?
  Then abundant thy supply!
He that goes most empty drinketh
  Deepest draughts of God's free grace,
For the "poor in spirit" only
  Is prepared the richest place.

—*Carrie F. Judd.*

Contents

Foreword *by Carrie Judd Montgomery* 1
Introduction 5

PART 1   A Life of Thirst 9

  1 Intersections 11
  2 Impact 15
  3 Carrie Judd Montgomery 19

PART 2   Writings by Carrie Judd Montgomery 29

  4 Rivers of Living Water 31
  5 Living Water 37
  6 Ocean Depths of Blessing 41
  7 Pentecostal Blessing 47
  8 Filled 51
  9 Living Waters 65
  10 The Promise of the Father.. 71
  11 The Life on Wings. 79

PART 3   Conversations 95

  12 A Conversation with Heidi Baker 99

PART 4   Spirit Flood 117

  13 Spirit Flood: Rebirth of Spirit Baptism
     for the 21st Century 121
Conclusion: Deeper Still 141
  About the Authors 145
  Further Resources 151
  Notes 157

Foreword

by Carrie Judd Montgomery

Come and Drink

One thought which was most helpful to us personally when we were seeking for the baptism of the Holy Ghost, is to be found in John 7:37, where Jesus stands and cries, saying, *"If any man thirst let him come unto to Me and drink."* How sweet to know that the thirsty ones, and only the thirsty ones are invited to come and drink of the living waters; and what is this thirst, but the longing which the Spirit of God Himself creates in the heart for His own incoming and indwelling? But the thirsty one is invited to come to the Lord Jesus and to drink, so that He says, *"He that believeth on Me… out of his inner being shall flow rivers of living water."* We are distinctly told that He is speaking this of the Spirit, but it is stated that it is by believing on Jesus that we receive the Holy Ghost. For while He is the promise of the Father, yet He is sent by the Father in the name of Jesus; and in John 16:7 Jesus says, "I will send Him unto you."

In our own personal experience the thirst created in our own soul for the Comforter's indwelling, was intense *beyond description*; one could only cry, "Lord Jesus, what is it to drink?" and again, "teach me to drink." How sweetly light was given, that the act of drinking is an act of faith. How quietly and yet how surely were we led to the definite faith which received at a certain moment the glorious Being who was henceforth to reveal Jesus to us in all His fullness; to guide into all truth; to comfort; to empower us as a witness. How real was the transaction; how satisfying the spiritual rest, as we believed that He had entered, though we had no special manifestation at the moment; how absolute was the faith that told Him we would always believe that He had at that moment taken possession of our whole being, whether He chose to manifest Himself in any remarkable way or not. Truly this was the inwrought faith of God Himself, and not any mere intellectual faith, which avails nothing. The Spirit Himself then led us to a quiet waiting at the feet of Jesus.

We have told in other writings of the gushing forth of those living waters six days later; of the marvelous manifestation; of His mighty presence; of every channel of our being placed at His disposal; of the blessed repose of mind; the holy quietness of brain and nerves; the "new tongues" which He voiced through us the fullness of worship and adoration to the glorious THREE IN ONE. We will not here speak further of this, but in a closing word will entreat the dear hungry and thirsty souls who have not yet received the fullness of their inheritance in Christ, to likewise come and drink; to give themselves over to the mighty searchlight of God Himself, that all things that hinder perfect belief may be purged away; thus faith shall spring spontaneously from Him who is the Author and Finisher of faith; for in addition to all that has been said, we must remember that God gives the Holy Ghost to those who obey Him.[2]

—CARRIE JUDD MONTGOMERY (1911)

Introduction

by Jennifer A. Miskov

Carrie Judd Montgomery (1858–1946) was a pioneering healing revivalist who had an unquenchable thirst for the fullness of the Holy Spirit all the days of her life. By stewarding the testimony of her miraculous healing in 1879, Carrie became an important catalyst and shaper of what is now known as the Divine Healing Movement. She had a profound ministry of healing and pioneered some of the earliest healing homes in our nation. Following her move to the West Coast, she opened the Home of Peace in Oakland, California, in 1893, which is still there to this day. In 1908 when she was fifty years old, she had her Pentecostal Spirit baptism experience with speaking in tongues. She later became a bridge between Evangelicalism and Pentecostalism and led many into their Spirit baptism experience as well as helped them to embrace divine healing.

Carrie's articles and books, mostly based on themes of healing, faith, unity in love, and hunger for more of God are saturated in the Holy Spirit. I spent four years studying her life and theology during my Ph.D. studies in England from 2007–2011. As I learned more about her and her relationship with God, I was profoundly inspired. My faith grew tremendously by reading her works. Her swiftness in responding to the Holy Spirit even when it didn't make sense quickened my heart. Her radical obedience led me to a place of deeper surrender and courage. Her testimonies provided strength for me when I was being led to step out in faith against all odds. Her hunger for more of God deepened my own longing for Him.

Because Carrie's writings had a significant impact on my life, God put it in my heart to make them readily accessible to others. *All Who Are Thirsty* is a sample of some of Carrie's works focusing on her hunger and thirst for the fullness of the Holy Spirit. I handpicked and transcribed select articles that first appeared in Carrie's *Triumphs of Faith* public periodical and one from her autobiography. To keep the text in its purest form, I have retained the original language and her italics. The grammatical mistakes have also been carried over from the original documents to preserve the authenticity of the text. The only minor changes I have made are slight punctuation corrections and the conversion of roman numerals to modern numbers. I believe that as you read this book, you, too, will discover hidden riches that will cause you to thirst more deeply for the rivers of living water.

This book is divided into four parts. In part one, I share how I first discovered Carrie and the impact she has had on my life. Included here is a short biography of her life that will give context to her writings. Part two is made up of select articles written by Carrie on the theme of the fullness of the Holy Spirit. These are presented in chronological order and span over thirty years of her life and ministry (from when she was twenty-three to fifty-three years old). Note that the term *Spirit baptism* when used after 1908 in her writing was influenced by the Pentecostal understanding of Spirit baptism that included speaking in tongues.

Part three is an interview I facilitated with Heidi Baker (Ph.D., founder of Iris Global, and missionary to Mozambique) about Carrie's legacy and passion for the fullness of the Holy Spirit. Creating dialogue between Carrie and Heidi, two of my spiritual mothers, invites us into a beautiful picture of weaving the old with the new to tap into the riches of the Holy Spirit over generations.

Part four is made up of an academic essay I previously published in a book entitled *Spirit Flood: Rebirth of Spirit Baptism for the 21st Century (In Light of the Azusa Street Revival and the Life of Carrie Judd Montgomery)*. By looking at Carrie's Spirit baptism experience, possible ways that Spirit baptism can re-emerge into the twenty-first century are explored.

Thank you for your courage to join me on this journey in *All Who Are Thirsty*. Jesus cried out on the last day of the feast, and continues to cry out today, for anyone who thirsts to come to Him and drink. As you respond to His call and drink deeply from Him as your true Source, may rivers of living water burst from within you.[3] As you tap into these pathways of old, may you find rest for your soul and access greater measures of the Spirit than ever before.[4]

—Jennifer A. Miskov, Ph.D.

PART 1
A Life of Thirst

I get the honor of introducing you to someone who has become a significant spiritual mother my journey. Though I have never met her personally, Carrie Judd Montgomery's impact on my life is significant and her legacy continues. She remained thirsty for more of the Holy Spirit throughout her entire life. As you get to know Carrie and learn how she cultivated a well of intimacy and encounter, may you, too, access greater rivers of living water.

Carrie Judd Montgomery in her Salvation Army
uniform when she was around thirty-four years old.
Photograph used by permission of the Flower Pentecostal Heritage Center.

1
Intersections

Revival. As Christians, we long for God to move among us in a powerful way. Over the years, I have seen many people encounter God in significant ways during revivals. But oftentimes during the years that follow, I have watched as some have retreated to their previous lifestyles—devoid of the promise and power that they had received. Many became disillusioned and disappeared from community. As this continued to happen, my heart broke more and more. I knew there must be a way to embrace all that God has during times of revival and to also carry that momentum forward.

It was in my heart to discover a model for sustainable revival. I wanted to learn how to effectively live through revivals and to carry that momentum forward into reformation. I wanted to know how to burn for Jesus without burning out. I dreamed about what it could look like to be passionate for Jesus in all seasons of life and for that flame of love to continue to burn more strongly the older I got.

So, in 2007, I took a leap of faith to explore the possibilities of seeing this dream become a reality. I quit my job, sold my car, and moved to England to study revival history. As I researched the great moves of God, I stumbled upon the story of a woman who fully embraced all that God had for her in several major moves of the Spirit *and* who continued to grow in her hunger for more of Him in the days that followed. I remember reading a small paragraph in my professor's book about a pioneering woman of faith who finished well. As I dug a little deeper, I realized that there was very little research done on her story other than a master's thesis completed twenty years earlier. I was drawn to learn more about her because of how she lived effectively through two major revivals *and* continued to increase in passion for Jesus as time went on. Because of her pioneering spirit, enduring faithfulness, and sustaining hunger for God, I decided to focus my Ph.D. research exclusively on her life, writings, and theology.

This divine intersection with Carrie happened when God sent me from the United States all the way over to England to discover a forgotten healing revivalist who had set up her ministry base in my home state of California. Little did I know that "meeting" Carrie through my research would radically impact my life and launch me into a greater measure of my destiny.

2
Impact

During my studies in England, as I read Carrie's teachings and learned more about her, I was impacted by her courageous faith and total surrender to God. In 1882 at twenty-three years old, she stepped out in radical obedience to pioneer one of the first healing homes in our nation with only a few months' rent to her name. This one act of faith helped catalyze healing homes across the nation during her time.

In February 2012, shortly after my return from studying in England, God led me to rent a house on Placer Street in Redding, California. I had only one month's rent to my name, and my situation felt impossible. But when I remembered Carrie's testimony of pioneering her healing home, I was encouraged in the Lord. If she could do it, then I believed I could trust in God in a radical way too. Her example ignited faith in me to put all my money into the security deposit and first month's rent and to trust in God. In the months following, He provided in miraculous and unusual ways. That one act of faith birthed what would later become known as Destiny House. This was the ministry I led there for seven years where we literally saw miracles, signs, and wonders take place in that home as we gathered around the presence of God to worship Him.[5]

Carrie also taught me how to be led by the Spirit, not by my circumstances. She taught me how to make decisions based upon God's truth rather than facts. I learned that if God initiates something, as I step out in faith to follow Him, He will work out all the details. I learned to understand at a deeper level that what God begins, He will complete (Philippians 1:6). If God calls me to go on a mission trip and I have no money, I learned from Carrie to step out in faith and to trust in Him. Through Carrie's inspiration, I followed my heart to venture to the San Francisco airport to get to my friend's wedding in England. Without any money or a plane ticket, I showed up by faith with only a small suitcase "packed" with testimonies of old. And praise God, He brought the breakthrough at the airport, and I was able to make it to her wedding.[6]

Another thing that has inspired me about Carrie's life is her sustaining and deepening hunger for more of God. Even after she had a successful healing ministry, at the age of fifty, Carrie was still open *and* hungry to step into the new move of God in her day. No matter how weird or controversial this new move of God appeared, she was willing to risk her reputation to take hold of all that God had for her. Even after she was baptized in the Spirit and spoke in tongues, her hunger to encounter God in even deeper measures continued to increase. No matter what experiences or encounters she had had in the past, if God was doing a new thing in her time, she was willing to dive all in. This inspires me with great hunger to pursue God no matter what it looks like today. It teaches me not to throw out the "baby with the bathwater" but to be patient and embrace all God is doing in revival times even if it comes through a package I might not expect or is offensive to me.

Carrie also taught me what it looks like to choose relationships above minor doctrinal differences and to pursue unity at all costs. Regardless of whether some of her friends spoke in tongues or not during the rise of early American Pentecostalism, that did not prevent Carrie from continuing to journey with them to advance the kingdom of God. She chose friendship first rather than being divided by denominational lines. This value for unity in love is crucial for today more than ever. Regardless of race, gender, or church affiliations, there is something to be said about covenanting together with our brothers and sisters for the unified cause to make Christ known and to see His glory poured out across the earth. Carrie did this incredibly well in many of the turbulent times she faced.

Carrie also taught me to understand the value and the power of the testimony. Every year on the anniversary of her healing, she would recount the story of her miraculous healing and give God thanks. In fact, the way she stewarded her testimony through writing and her ministry was catalytic to shift Evangelicalism from believing God wanted people "to endure suffering with a good attitude" to embrace the truth that "God wants to, and does, heal today." Whenever we share a testimony, it acts as a prophetic revelation and invitation for God to do again what He did before. In the sharing of testimonies, something powerful is unlocked. Releasing testimonies has become a key component in my own life and ministry because of what I learned from Carrie. As a result, I have seen many people led into life-changing encounters with God by following in the footsteps of Carrie in this way.

So now, without further ado, I have the privilege to introduce you to a spiritual mother and friend whom I have never personally met but have grown to deeply value in my life. May her story enrich your life as it has done mine, and increase your thirst for more of the Spirit.

3
Carrie Judd Montgomery

Carrie Judd Montgomery (1858–1946) was a pioneer of the faith who paved the way for many to follow, especially in relation to divine healing and Spirit baptism.[7] Throughout her life and ministry, Carrie burned for Jesus but never burned out. She cultivated an enduring pursuit of the fullness of the Holy Spirit till the day she died. Her unrelenting spiritual hunger for God led her into deep encounters that she regularly shared with others to encourage them to journey to the same depths.

Following a long season of sickness, Carrie was launched into her healing ministry. In 1876, in her hometown of Buffalo, New York, Carrie fell hard on the icy ground on her walk to school. She severely damaged her spine, which later resulted in tuberculosis of the spine and then of the blood. This developed into hyperesthesia where she was bedridden for two years, very near death.

In 1879, her father read a testimony in the public newspaper of an African American woman named Sarah Ann Freeman Mix who was healed of tuberculosis. Carrie's family immediately wrote to Mrs. Mix asking for prayer. Carrie received a response from Mrs. Mix a few days later with guidelines in how to position herself for healing. She wrote Carrie telling her that she would pray in her home in Connecticut at a certain time a few days later. She exhorted Carrie to do the same and then to act in faith regardless of how she felt. Then on February 26, 1879, when they both had set aside time to pray, Carrie prayed the prayer of faith found in James 5 and got out of bed by faith. This began her healing process and eventually catapulted her into a lifelong ministry of healing.

Many were healed by God when they heard the story of Carrie's miracle. She ended up publishing her testimony of healing in a book entitled *The Prayer of Faith*, released in 1880. It became one of the earlier theological presentations on divine healing and healing in the atonement. By 1893, more than forty thousand copies were in print. It was also translated into several languages and distributed around the world. During Carrie's lifetime and since, many people have attested to being healed as they read her testimony.

In 1881, Carrie launched a significant holiness periodical called *Triumphs of Faith*. She edited the publication until her death and often wrote articles under the simple title "the editor." This periodical became a major communication tool that spread healing testimonies and revival fires around the world. It also provided a platform to launch women in ministry at a time when this was faced with great resistance.

Carrie's early eagerness to release her testimony of healing with people outside as well as inside her Episcopalian tradition immediately set her on a path to have an ecumenical impact. She soon became a part of the formation of the Christian and Missionary Alliance denomination of churches and was close friends with its founder, A. B. Simpson. Even though it was uncommon for women to preach, Carrie would regularly share her testimony of healing wherever doors opened to her. At times, she even got kicked out of churches because she was a woman preacher, spoke to African Americans, or shared the controversial message of healing.

Carrie also opened some of the earliest healing homes in the nation beginning with one in Buffalo, New York in 1881. During this time in Evangelicalism, many people believed that if one was sick, the best way to honor God was to patiently endure suffering with a good attitude. But because Carrie believed God is good and His heart is to heal, she opened a room in her home to receive those in need of healing. There, she would teach them about healing and pray for them. Because it was not acceptable to teach about healing in churches during this time, desperate ones would travel to healing homes where they could learn about and pray for healing in a safe space.

In 1890, Carrie married George Montgomery who relocated her from New York to California. As a result of her move, she was one of the first people to spread divine healing themes to the West Coast. She continued her healing home ministry by opening the Home of Peace in Oakland, California, officially dedicating it on November 7, 1893. This became the first healing home on the West Coast, with its doors opening nearly twenty years before John G. Lake's healing rooms launched in 1913.

The timing of Carrie's healing was pivotal for Evangelicalism to be open to embrace divine healing. Her testimony, literature, and ministry acted as a tipping point to shift people from a belief that God's will is for people to patiently endure suffering, to the realization that God's heart is for all to be healed. Significant apostolic leaders such as A. J. Tomlinson, Francisco Olazábal, and others gained insight and then embraced divine healing as being for today through Carrie's diverse ministry.

Carrie also started orphanages, was involved in evangelistic work, and initiated camp meetings in Cazadero, California that drew together people from various traditions. In several historical accounts of the Divine Healing Movement, she is the only woman listed among other key shapers—the lists often include Charles Cullis, A. B. Simpson, A. J. Gordon, William E. Boardman, Andrew Murray, and Carrie. Before the turn of the century, because of her husband's personal ties with William and Catherine Booth, Carrie and George also became honorary officers in the Salvation Army.

On April 9, 1906, the Azusa Street Revival in Los Angeles, California was ignited and began to spread like wildfire.[8] Carrie began to hear testimonies from friends who had been baptized in the Holy Spirit in conjunction with this new move of God. In 1908, at the age of fifty and having already become a successful minister, Carrie made time to explore what was at the heart of this revival. Regardless of any previous experiences or ministry platforms, Carrie was vigilant to take hold of all that God had for her in her generation. She set out to meet and pray with others who had had their Pentecostal Spirit baptism experience, so she could also experience the same overflow. She describes her journey in an article titled "'The Promise of the Father.' A Personal Testimony." Carrie's subsequent Pentecostal experience with speaking in tongues deepened her spirituality, and from that moment forward, Pentecostal themes and testimonies became integrated into her periodical.

Following this experience, Carrie could have become settled in her pursuit of God, feeling that she had already arrived. But instead, she continued to long for even greater measures of the Holy Spirit. She tells about this increasing desire in a sermon entitled "Life on Wings: The Possibilities of Pentecost." Throughout the years, the encounters Carrie had intensified her hunger to seek for more of the Holy Spirit.

In 1909, Carrie embarked upon a missionary tour to China, India, and Great Britain. Because of her established reputation within the Divine Healing Movement, she was able to introduce many Evangelicals to the Pentecostal Spirit baptism experience. For early Pentecostals, she was also able to bring balance in the midst of the fanaticism associated with the gift of speaking in tongues. Her radical Evangelicalism mixed with moderate Pentecostalism enabled her to have a respected voice within both movements and act as a bridge to bring them closer together.

Historians over the years have referred to Carrie as a poet, early itinerant preacher, long-range curer (because she prayed for the sick from a distance), philanthropist, editor, faith healer, radical Evangelical, pioneer—and even the first Charismatic. She truly was a Pentecostal pioneer of the faith who impacted many significant apostolic leaders of her day. She also brought revolutionary shifts to Evangelicalism and opened the door for women preachers to arise. Carrie was not only one of the most influential people in the North American Divine Healing Movement, but she also played a significant role in the growth and expansion of the early Pentecostal Movement.

✳Though Carrie eventually joined the Assemblies of God in its early formation, she continued to transcend denominational barriers and never cut ties with her previous connections. Her association with groups such as the Salvation Army, Christian and Missionary Alliance, and then later the Assemblies of God never closed her off from sharing what God had done in her life with people outside of these affiliations. <u>This was possible because she was more concerned with building relationships and freely giving away all she had received rather than being consumed with building ministry platforms.</u> <u>Many of these relationships were formed as she joined various movements in their initial phases before power structures could be crystallized.</u> Through her relational network, she influenced many from different backgrounds to embrace all that God had for them, even if it was unfamiliar or unpopular.

Carrie was friends with many prominent Christian leaders in her time such as Minnie Abrams, Elizabeth Baxter, Alexander A. Boddy, William Booth, Charles Cullis, John G. Lake, Aimee Semple McPherson, Pandita Ramabai, William J. Seymour, A. B. Simpson, Maria Woodworth-Etter, Smith Wigglesworth, and others. Because she was so young at the time she was healed, she was one of the few leaders who brought theological roots from the Holiness Movement into Pentecostalism.[9]

Carrie continued her ministry until her death on July 26, 1946, and was succeeded by her only child, Faith Berry. The Home of Peace in Oakland is still open to this day and remains in line with her original vision. Moreover, the stewardship of her testimonies through her writings continues to release healing today.

Carrie continually gave away whatever she received from God. After her healing, she shared her testimony and prayed for others to be made well. She later lived through the Pentecostal revival of the early 1900s where she was open *and* hungry for all the Spirit wanted to do, while remaining balanced in the midst of fanaticism. The way in which she approached revivals and newer moves of God with an open heart to receive all that He had for her serves to encourage people today to do the same. After her Pentecostal Spirit baptism experience, she encouraged others to move toward the same fullness. Whenever she experienced something from God (healing, Spirit baptism, or another breakthrough), she eagerly sought to help others receive the same blessing. She never tried to convert or recruit others to her ministry or affiliations. She simply wanted them to experience the fullness of the Holy Spirit as she had.

Regardless of Carrie's previous ministry successes, she remained hungry for God throughout her lifetime. She also was faithful to her husband and to the Lord all the days of her life. Though she had faults like we all do today, she strived to live a life of total surrender to the Holy Spirit. She walked in unity with love when it was challenging, hungered for the fullness of the Spirit even if it looked messy, walked in power for healing when it was controversial, and remained full of faith even when it didn't make sense. Carrie serves as an inspiration, not only for women to step out in faith against all odds but for all people to live fully surrendered to the Holy Spirit.

No matter what incredible encounters or ministry successes one already has had, Carrie's passion for more of God throughout her lifetime demonstrates that there is always more of the Holy Spirit to discover. This invitation to dive deeper into the limitless oceans of God's presence awaits *all who are thirsty.*

This photo was taken at one of Carrie's Cazadero camp meetings in California where hungry ones would gather to seek more of God. Many times people never made it to the main sessions because they were laid out, slain in the Spirit in Carrie's tent. The blurred child in the middle is Carrie's daughter, Faith, and the tall man with the hat on the far right is Carrie's husband, George. Photograph used by permission of the Berry family (Carrie's grandchildren and great-grandchildren).

Part 2
Writings by Carrie Judd Montgomery

Carrie accessed hidden spiritual streams available to all Christians. In part two, we will now dive into her inner spiritual life as she shares about the fullness of and her experiences with the Holy Spirit over a span of thirty years. We start with an article she wrote when she was twenty-three years old and end with one she released in her early fifties. In her upcoming article "Rivers of Living Water," she writes, "Shall we continue to cry with thirst when by an act of simple faith we may drink of its abundant outflow?" Rather than thirsting to death while sitting under the waterfall of His presence, Carrie urges us to drink of the spiritual things we have *already* freely been given.

As you tap into the secret currents in Carrie's life, you will gain access to these same streams. The deeper realms of the Holy Spirit that Carrie accessed are freely available to each one of us. As you read, I encourage you to take in her words slowly and ponder deeply what the Spirit might be saying to you today.

TRIUMPHS OF FAITH.

A MONTHLY JOURNAL.

Now thanks be unto God, which always causeth us to triumph in Christ.—II Corinthians ii. 14.

Vol. 15.   JULY, 1895.   No. 7.

FILLED.

BY THE EDITOR.

[An address delivered at the Sunday morning service, Home of Peace. Reported by Miss Cecilia Decker.]

LAST night the word "filled" kept coming to me over and over again, as I thought of that text "filled with the fruits of righteousness," and then this morning I was asking the Lord for a message and it came again to me, "*filled.*" So I looked up a few of the many passages on that subject, and the Lord has given me some very precious texts that have already been a great blessing to my own heart and I know that they will be a blessing to you also if you will just take them in. The Lord wants you to be *filled*—He does not want you to be half full, but brim full, and then every fresh drop that comes from Heaven into your soul will keep you overflowing.

The first text is in Psalm lxxxi. 10: "I am the Lord thy God which brought thee out of the land of Egypt: open thy mouth wide, and I will fill it." Now you see here the conditions of the filling in these words. You see what you must do in order to get the great blessing that God has in His heart for you. "*Open thy mouth wide*, and I will *fill* it." Now, in this figure of speech the Lord simply means for you to let your soul be wide open. The natural mouth is

This is a sample issue of what a *Triumphs of Faith* periodical looked like. "The Editor" refers to Carrie Judd Montgomery as the author.

4
Rivers of Living Water

Carrie Judd Montgomery
(April 1881)

He cutteth out rivers among the rocks.
—Job 28:10

I know that there are many dear ones thirsting to-day for more of the "water of life," and crying in the words of the Psalmist, "As the hart panteth after the water brooks, so panteth my soul after Thee, O God."

Precious, indeed, is the answer which our pitiful Father vouchsafes to His weary children, "I will pour water upon him that is thirsty, and floods upon the dry ground: I will pour My Spirit upon thy seed, and My blessing upon thine offspring." –(Isa. 44:3).

Such an outpouring of God's Spirit as is here promised is essential to every believer before he can work with power in the service of the Lord: for we cannot give what we do not possess, and we cannot water others unless we, ourselves, are drawing from the Living Fountain. Blessed be God, He "giveth not the Spirit by measure" unto those who will open their hearts to receive Him. It is not His will that we should be limited to occasional dews of His grace, but His unbounded mercy reveals itself in the promise of "*floods*" of blessing "upon the dry ground."

And why then are we not filled? Why are we not so full of the blessed Spirit of God that His fullness can flow through us, and out of us, refreshing our own souls and all those with whom we come in contact? Alas! we will not take the receptive attitude of faith. Jesus bids us "ask and receive" that our "joy may be full." We obey His command in *asking*, but we do not throw open our souls that we may *receive*. God's word to us is, "Open thy mouth wide, and I will fill it" (Psa. 81:10), yet we do not pause in our cries of hunger to accept what is so freely offered.

The mistake that very many of us make is in asking God to give us holiness of heart as though it were something apart from Himself. We do not realize that Jesus has already been given to us by the Father, and that our possession of His attributes consists only in our possessing Him: "A Man shall be....as rivers of water in a dry place." –(Isa. 32:2).

This "Man," Christ Jesus, when "He bore our sins in His own body on the tree" knew what it was to suffer thirst; though He was, and is, the "Living fountain." He thirsted for our sakes that we might be made to "drink of the river of His pleasures." We hear Him saying those words of patient grief, "They gave Me also gall for my meat; and in My thirst they gave Me vinegar to drink" (Psa. 69:21), and then in vivid contrast with man's mocking cruelty we hear the Saviour's message of matchless grace: "When the poor and needy seek water and there is none; and their tongue faileth for thirst, I, the Lord will hear them, I the God of Israel will not forsake them, I will open rivers in high places, and fountains in the midst of the valleys; I will make the wilderness a pool of water and the dry land springs of water." –(Isa. 41:17, 18).

The "cold flowing waters" (Jer. 18:14) never cease in their beneficent action. They are available for us at all times if we will only receive them, but we must drink by faith. Jesus has said, "If any man thirst let him come unto Me and drink," and the utterance of faith would be, "Lord Jesus, I *come*, and according to Thy word I do *drink now.*" And depending on that unfailing word we may rest in the sure conviction that marvelous refreshing will be shed abroad in our souls by that living draught. "The glorious Lord will be unto us a place of broad rivers and streams." –(Isa. 33:21). Not only shall our own souls be abundantly satisfied, but "rivers of living water" shall flow from us to the reviving of other thirsty souls, and they, and we, shall show forth the praise of the Lord; for "unto the place from whence the rivers come, thither they return again." –(Eccl. 1:7).

In Isa. 48:21, we read, "He caused the waters to flow out of the rock for them: He clave the rock also, and the waters gushed out." Dear friends, the Rock has already been cleft for us, and the spiritual drink of love and peace is even now *gushing out* to satisfy our every need. Shall we in our impatience and unbelief "smite the Rock" which is so ready to satisfy our longing that a single word of appeal shall enable us to partake of its "living waters"? Shall we continue to cry with thirst when by an act of simple faith we may drink of its abundant outflow? Let us beware lest in our disobedience and lack of trust we fall short of the end of our service, and hear the rebuking words, "Because ye believed Me not, to sanctify Me in the eyes of the children of Israel, therefore ye shall not bring this congregation into the land which I have given them."–(Num. 20:12).

If we have not wherewith to water the fainting souls around us, shall we not be held accountable by our Master for the unfruitfulness of our service? We read that at the last day the Judge of all the earth shall say unto the unprofitable servants, "I was thirsty and ye gave me no drink... Inasmuch as ye did it not unto one of the least of these, ye did it not unto Me."–(St. Matt. 25:42, 45). Solemn words that we should ponder well! For if we fail to drink deeply of Christ's spiritual drink we shall be without excuse, inasmuch as the gracious invitation is even now sounding in our ears, "Let him that is athirst come. And whosoever will, let him take the water of life freely."–(Rev. 22:17).

Are we *"athirst"*? Then we are invited to drink of this living water, and let us partake so freely that those who have not yet known a "thirst after righteousness" may realize by our fullness their own lack, and be constrained to *"ask and receive."*

"Ho every one that thirsteth come ye to the waters."–(Isa. 55:1).

"Whosoever drinketh of the water that I shall give him shall never thirst; but the water that I shall give him shall be in him a well of water springing up into everlasting life."–(St. John 4:14).[10]

5
Living Water

Carrie Judd Montgomery
(March 1887)

"I will pour water upon him that is thirsty, and floods upon the dry ground; I will pour My Spirit upon thy seed, and My blessing upon thine offspring; and they shall spring up as among the grass, as willows by the water-courses."

If you are thirsting for God, yea, for the living God, then this promise is for you. You need not be discouraged because of your thirst, but rather you may be encouraged, because the blessing is only held out to "him that is thirsty." The invitation reads, "Let him that is athirst come. And whosoever will, let him take the water of life freely," and again in the same chapter we find the definite promise, "I will give unto him that is athirst of the fountain of the water of life freely."

Thus, you see, dear thirsting soul, that you need not longer thirst, for there is the sound of abundance of water, of which you may freely partake.

The Lord Jesus had pronounced those blessed who thirst after righteousness, and He has allowed to come to you the utter dissatisfaction with all human springs, in order that you may seek after living water to satisfy your thirsty soul. You have indeed proved that those who drink from earthly wells shall thirst again, and now you are ready to hear the voice of Jesus as He calls, "If any man thirst let him come unto Me and drink." "Whosoever drinketh of the water that I shall give him shall never thirst; but the water that I shall give him shall be in him a well of water springing up into everlasting life."

Shall not your response be, "Lord, give *me* this water, that I thirst not?" Then shall you not only be filled yourself, but streams of living water shall flow forth from your heart, to refresh and bless other thirsty lives. And that we might not be left in any doubt as to what was meant by this water of life, it is recorded, "This spake He of the Spirit which they that believe on Him should receive." The invitation is given in a very broad sense, so you cannot be left out. "Ho, *every one* that thirsteth, come ye to the waters." You need not, must not bring money or price for the gift of God cannot be bought, and the one called is "he that hath no money." So you cannot be too needy to come. The more needy you are, the more right you have to this invitation. The needy ones are especially mentioned in Isa. 41:17, 18, "When the poor and needy seek water, and there is none, and their tongues faileth for thirst, I the Lord, will hear them, I the God of Israel, will not forsake them. I will open rivers in high places, and fountains in the midst of the valleys; I will make the wilderness a pool of water, and the dry land springs of water." Even when "their tongues fail for thirst," when they can no longer make a cry or a moan, yet the Lord hears them. And why does He notice so quickly our failing lips and parched spirits? Ah, have you forgotten that scene on Calvary, when the crucified One said with failing tongue, "*I thirst*"? And in the prophetic record we read the moan of agony, "I looked for some to take pity, but there was none; and for comforters, but I found none. They gave Me also gall for My meat; and in My thirst they gave Me vinegar to drink." The blessed Saviour thirsted that *we* might not thirst, and therefore He waits to pour floods of living water – the fullness of His lifegiving spirit, upon all who are fainting and longing for Him. The rock has already been smitten, and we have only now to "*speak* unto the rock" to bring forth the waters of life. –(Num. 20:8).

God grant, dear reader, that you may constantly drink that "spiritual drink," even as it is recorded of God's ancient people, "they drank of that spiritual Rock that went with them and that Rock was Christ."

"They thirsted not when He led them through the deserts; He caused the waters to flow out of the Rock for them; He clave the Rock also, and the water gushed out."[11]

6
Ocean Depths of Blessing, and Further Service

Carrie Judd Montgomery
(1880s)

*The following encounter happened sometime in the 1880s and was written about in her biography in 1936.

As I went on with the Lord I felt an unspeakable hunger springing up within me for more of God. I hardly knew how to pray, but would sometimes turn to my Heavenly Father and say to Him, "What dost *Thou* want?"; because it seemed to me it was more His desire to obtain full possession of me than my desire for Himself. Previously I have spoken of the great blessing I received when I was healed, and my consciousness that the Holy Spirit had come to abide with me. Now, it seemed that He was longing to get full control of me and to fill the temple although I scarcely knew how to put this into words.

While still feeling this great hunger after more of God, I heard of Christian people farther East who had had a great anointing from the Lord and my heart cried out for fellowship with these dear people. I heard much about one sister who lived a very victorious life, and who was much used of God in His work. The Christian woman [this was likely Mary H. Mossman] had a Home in New Jersey, where she entertained those who were waiting on the Lord for a deeper spiritual life and for healing of the body. I got in touch with her and made arrangements to go to her for a little stay. I well remember how my hunger seemed to deepen more and more even while I was on the train journeying from Buffalo to this sister's place of residence.

When I arrived at the Home I was met in the most affectionate and motherly way by this dear saint, who informed me, after she had given me her welcome, that the evening meal was just about ready. My reply to her was as follows:

"Oh, I do not want anything to eat; I want God."

She had herself, been led into depths and heights of spiritual blessing, so she thoroughly sympathized with me in the desire which I thus expressed. She left me alone in the upper room waiting on God, while she looked after some household duties, and then she returned to me. We knelt quietly together and I do not remember that there was much, if any, audible prayer by either of us, but the presence of the Lord became more and more manifest as we continued our worship together.

All at once I experienced a blessing that is difficult to put into words. It seemed as though God manifested Himself in a cloud of Heavenly dew which descended gently upon my head and entered into my being, taking full possession of me. At the same time a sweet, restful feeling almost overpowered me so that my own strength somewhat left me and I leaned over and rested my head upon this sister's shoulder. No words were given me, but the dear one by my side seemed to be so one with me that she fully understood the cloud of glory into which I was entering, for His presence seemed to surround me, and at the same time to fill me.

After a little while something called my friend away from my side, and I lay down upon a bed in the room, still feeling the wonderful presence of the Lord and silently adoring Him. While waiting on the Lord a few more days in this hallowed Home, the manifestation of the Lord's presence about me, and within me, became still more glorious until my whole being seemed to be filled with "rivers of living water" and Jesus Himself revealed as the One among ten thousand, the Lily of the Valley.

I was so conscious that my body, as well as my soul, became so hallowed with the Lord's presence that I was made to realize as never before that I was indeed a temple of the Holy Ghost. The Life of God came even into my tongue; not that my tongue moved, but I could feel the moving of God's life distinctly through that member of my body. I was held silent in adoration of the glorious Being who was thus revealed to me, conscious of great joy in His immediate presence, and especially delighting in the thought of entire yieldedness to His perfect will. The only part of my body which did not seem to partake of the infilling was my head, and I believe this was because I was still a little self-conscious and desiring to keep a little human touch upon myself lest I should, in this great tidal blessing, drift too far out to sea. Many years later I received a still greater enduement of power, and at that time the last bit of human reserve on my part was taken away and God had complete possession of His temple. But this experience will be spoken of more fully at another time.

On my way home on the train I had occasion to speak to a lady about her soul and great anointing was upon me as I talked to her, such as I had never experienced before.

When I reached my home I quietly confided to my dear mother my joyful experience, and she praised God with me. The power of God continued to rest upon me in my meetings so that it was told me by one of my friends that it was quite noticeable to others who attended the meetings that I had received an anointing which they had never discerned in me before. The Word of God became more and more precious and it was opened to me increasingly as I expounded it to others.[12]

7
Pentecostal Blessing

Carrie Judd & George Montgomery
(March 1895)

Our Home of Peace keeps full most of the time with those who need help either in soul or body. It has proved to be the very gate of heaven to many weary souls; tired Christian workers have here renewed their strength, sick bodies have been healed and hungry hearts have been filled with waves of peace for which they were longing.

While I was absent from Home during the past week holding special meetings in the Salvation Army, an unusual wave of glory visited the Home of Peace and a description of this blessed meeting was sent me in a private letter which I received from my dear husband. I feel constrained to take extracts from this letter for the benefit of my readers as I believe they will be interested to know of the blessings that the Lord is pouring upon this sweet Home so given up to His service. I quote from my husband's letter as follows:

"Hallelujah! Last night we had the most wonderful time ever known in Beulah, in fact, ever experienced by any one present. God opened the flood gates of Heaven and poured us out such a blessing that there was not room enough to contain it. He filled us with the joy of Heaven. The Holy Ghost was so noticeably present that we could not stand much more of the glory. We asked, what must Heaven be if God could give us so much of it down here on this earth. It came very unexpectedly upon us; we were not going to have much of a meeting. Miss B— read the lesson and prayed, and then left us and took Mrs. H— the sick lady up to bed, but while some of the others were praying the Holy Ghost descended in mighty power melting all of us down under His incoming presence. Such a meeting could not be described and will never be forgotten by any present either here or throughout Eternity, for God so manifestly revealed Himself unto us.

We had wonderful liberty in prayer not only for all Beulah, but for all the people in this neighborhood, and then praying for one and another as the Holy Spirit brought different ones to our remembrance. Special liberty was given in prayer for your mission in Napa Valley, we believe that the Holy Ghost will use you as the channel through which He shall pour the living waters. Keep low; keep out of sight. The Holy Ghost wants clean and mighty vessels. He will do the work, not you. Not by might or by power, but by His Spirit. Oh, how this was realized last night! As we counted up the number present we found that there were just twelve and Jesus in the midst. When it would seem as though the blessing were passing another still mightier wave would come over us, and the exultation and praise that went up to Heaven was wonderful and beautiful.

When I went up to my room I saw it was half past one this morning, and then I felt as though I could not bear to go to sleep. Jesus was so manifestly present. He talked with me and I could see Him in a wonderful, real way, as never before. The Word was illuminated under this mighty baptism of the Holy Spirit, and I understood it better than ever before. Oh, I am sure that it is our privilege not to be half full, but to be *filled to overflowing*, and *that all the time*, and the overflowing rivers will then be poured out to a thirsty, lost world. Well, I can never get through telling you so I will have to wait till you return, if we do not meet in the air before the week is over. Last night many of us felt that a little more of this glory in our souls would have translated us. We were all like a lot of people drunk with new wine of the Kingdom. Hallelujah! Hallelujah."[13]

Photographs of the Home of Peace in Oakland, California used by permission of Jennifer A. Miskov.

8
Filled

Carrie Judd Montgomery
(July 1895)

*This is taken from a Sunday morning sermon
Carrie preached at Home of Peace.

L ast night the word "filled" kept coming to me over and over again, as I thought of that text "filled with the fruits of righteousness," and then this morning I was asking the Lord for a message and it came again to me, *"filled."* So I looked up a few of the many passages on that subject, and the Lord has given me some very precious texts that have already been a great blessing to my own heart and I know that they will be a blessing to you also if you will just take them in. The Lord wants you to be *filled* – He does not want you to be half full, but brim full, and then every fresh drop that comes from Heaven into your soul will keep you overflowing.

The first text is in Psalm 81:10: "I am the Lord thy God which brought thee out of the land of Egypt: open thy mouth wide, and I will fill it." Now you see here the conditions of the filling in these words. You see what you must do in order to get the great blessing that God has in His heart for you. "*Open thy mouth wide*, and I will *fill* it." Now, in this figure of speech the Lord simply means for you to let your soul be wide open. The natural mouth is given you to take in food with; now let your soul be like a great mouth. Let your whole spirit open up to God this morning. He just wants the emptiness into which to pour His fullness. He wants you to be all ready to receive His blessing. "Open your mouth '*wide*,'" He says. Perhaps you have opened it a little; that shows you expect a small mouthful. Do as the children do when you have a big piece of candy for them – they will open their mouths very wide to take it in. Now God has a big blessing for your soul and you can have just as much of it as you will take. If you have the faith to open your mouth wide this morning, He will surely fill it.

Something else about this "filling." Let us turn to Exodus 40:34, 35. We read in this chapter about the tabernacle being reared and how everything was put in readiness. When everything was in its place, and the whole thing completed, we read, "Then a cloud covered the tent of the congregation, and the glory of the Lord *filled* the tabernacle. And Moses was not able to enter into the tent of the congregation, because the cloud abode thereon, and the glory of the Lord *filled* the tabernacle."

When anything is full it cannot hold more, and the "glory of the Lord filled the tabernacle," so there was not room even for Moses. Even that blessed man of God could not enter. Oh, how glorious to realize that there is not any room for self to enter when the glory of the Lord fills the tabernacle. Moses was a type of the law, and the old law is put out and the new law comes in. You know the new law of our life is the Spirit of the Lord; "the law of the Spirit of Life in Christ Jesus hath made us free from the law of sin and death." The old law is abolished, and the new law of life and victory and glory is brought in by the presence of God Himself, by the abiding of the Holy Ghost.

There is a wonderful verse in Exodus 29:43, "And there I will meet the children of Israel, and the tabernacle shall be sanctified by My glory. And I will sanctify the tabernacle of the congregation, and the altar; I will sanctify also both Aaron and his sons, to minister to Me in the priest's office."

Where did He say He would meet with them? Why, at the *door* of the tabernacle, where there was a "continual burnt offering." The "continual burnt offering" shows forth the sacrifice of Jesus Christ, and He is the door as well as the sacrifice, and right there He meets with us, and He says the tabernacle shall be "sanctified by My glory." What high honor has God put upon us? He says, "Ye are the temple of the living God," and you, beloved, are the tabernacle of the Lord this morning. You are to be *sanctified* by His glory. He is meeting with us through Christ this morning, and He wants to come in and fill you, like that tabernacle of olden time, that you may be sanctified by His glorious presence. If you will let Him fill you with the power of His Spirit, you will know what sanctification means, and you will not then have a little bit of salvation that can barely keep your soul alive, but you will get such glory from the Lord that you cannot hold any more at times, and the old man will be put out so he never can go in any more, and the glory of the Lord will keep the temple.

Also in Leviticus 16:2 there is such a sweet word: "And the Lord said unto Moses, Speak unto Aaron thy brother, that he come not at all times into the holy place within the vail before the mercy seat, which is upon the ark; that he die not; for I will appear in the cloud upon the mercy seat." Ah, that is where He appears in the cloud of glory, on the Mercy Seat.

"There is a place where spirits blend,
Where friend finds fellowship with friend,
A place than all beside more sweet,
It is the blood-bought Mercy Seat."

Oh, how precious it is, that right there at the Mercy Seat Christ not only meets us, but we meet with each other. No soul can touch another soul in nature, but in grace all souls are one. We wander "in a solitary way" until we know the grace of God, and then we come into the City of the New Jerusalem, into the heavenly Zion, and find our citizenship is in heaven, and we are joined to all the saints in Heaven and the saints on earth. The Mercy Seat speaks to us of the sacrifice of our Lord Jesus Christ, and there God appears in the cloud of glory. You are His temple and He wants you to be filled with glory. Why, you did not know that, did you? You thought it would be time enough to be filled with glory when you died and went to Heaven, but you need not wait, for He will let the glory right down from Heaven into your souls.

Turn to 1 Kings 8:10, 11: "And it came to pass, when the priests were come out of the holy place, that the cloud filled the house of the Lord, so that the priests could not stand to minister because of the cloud; for the glory of the Lord had filled the house of the Lord." This was when Solomon had finished the building of the temple; everything was complete and then he called all the people together for the dedication of the temple. And so when you get ready to dedicate yourselves to God in a solemn, definite way, in the presence of the people, there will happen to you spiritually just what happened in that temple in older times. Are you ready to dedicate yourself to-day – spirit, soul and body? Then the Holy Ghost will come and take possession of His temple. He always takes possession of all who are fully yielded, but sometimes there is some little portion that is kept back. "Lord you may have all the other rooms in the temple, but I am going to keep that one for my private use." And then we wonder why the cloud of glory does not come! "Lord you can have all the rest of the house, but I am going to reserve one little portion for my glory." And then we wonder that the glory of the Lord does not come! He says, "I will not give My glory to another." And yet, when all the house is given up to His occupation, you shall behold and taste His glory. "The priests could not stand to minister because of the cloud; for the glory of the Lord had filled the house of the Lord."

Now remember the two words "glory" and "filled," which we find so frequently in this Bible reading. Oh, just be ready this morning for the filling, and the filling brings the glory, and then you yourself will not stand to minister any more. You have been trying in the past to minister to the Lord and have made poor work of it, but when the cloud of glory fills the house, the Great High Priest comes in, and He says, "You must stand aside and I will do the ministering." Praise God, He ministers in us and through us, and causes us to become kings and priests unto God.

Look next at 2 Chronicles, 5:13, 14: "It came even to pass, as the trumpeters and singers were as one, to make one sound to be heard in praising and thanking the Lord; and when they lifted up their voice with the trumpets and cymbals and instruments of music, and praised the Lord, saying, 'For He is good, for His mercy endureth for ever,' that then the house was filled with a cloud, even the house of the Lord; so that the priests could not stand to minister by reason of the cloud: for the glory of the Lord had filled the house of God."

This is another record of the same occurrence, but in this record the Holy Ghost has shown us plainly what the people were doing when the cloud filled the house; they were making their voices as one in praise. There was one clash of trumpets and cymbals, and instruments and human voices, and all through the places there was the voice of praise, and then the God of glory filled the house. Now, this is a wonderful lesson for us. When everything within us unites to praise the Lord then He will come with a cloud of glory and fill the house. Some of you have prayed many times and wondered why the glory cloud did not drop down upon you, but then at last the Spirit showed you that you had to change your attitude from prayer to praise, and had to take by faith the position of victory, and as you began to praise Him by faith before you saw the cloud, and before you felt it, all at once the cloud of glory dropped down upon you and your prayers were more than answered. Is it not so?

Also look at the 7th chapter of the same book, first and second verses: "Now when Solomon had made an end of praying, the fire came down from Heaven, and consumed the burnt offering and the sacrifices; and the glory of the Lord filled the house. And the priests could not enter into the house of the Lord, because the *glory of the Lord had filled the Lord's house.* And when all the children of Israel saw how the fire came down, and the glory of the Lord upon the house, they bowed themselves with their faces to the ground upon the pavement, and worshipped and praised the Lord, saying, 'For He is good; for His mercy endureth forever.'"

Now first notice in chapter 6:41 that God had an invitation to come in before He came. "Arise, O Lord unto Thy resting place." The Lord's resting place is in your heart. Oh, think of it, and He wants you to invite Him into His resting place. He will come to rest there if you will invite Him and open the door for Him to come in. The Lord's portion is His people, and Jacob is the lot of His inheritance.

Then the fire came down from Heaven because the sacrifices were all ready. They were all on the altar and ready to be consumed or the fire would never have come down. Get your sacrifices ready, beloved, lay the wood in order, get all on the altar, and then trust Him for the fire, and when the fire comes down to consume the sacrifices the glory of the Lord shall fill the house.

Now, evidently, there were two classes; there were the people that were praising the Lord *before* the fire fell, and before the glory came. They were the people of faith; they were the Lord's own priests; but here is another class of the children of Israel who "*saw* how the fire came down," and then they bowed themselves and praised the Lord, and said: "He is good." They did not know how to praise Him before till they *saw*, but I tell you it is a good thing to let the fire come down in us, and the glory, so that people outside *can* see. O God, let the tabernacle of our souls be so filled with the glory of the Lord that the people who will not believe any other way will see it and bow themselves before Thee!

Now, I will take some passages in the New Testament. Luke 1:53: "He hath filled the hungry with good things; and the rich He hath sent empty away." It is the hungry people that He fills. If any one comes already filled He sends them away and their fullness is only emptiness, because it is not of Heaven's fullness. Is your soul hungry for the baptism of the Holy Ghost? If so, then he is ready to fill you.

We read again in Matthew 5:6, that sweet word so blessed to seeking souls in every generation: "Blessed are they which do hunger and thirst after righteousness, for they shall be filled." This means that even while you are hungering after the Holy Spirit, God counts you blessed. O blessed Hunger, put in us by the Holy Spirit, and sure to be satisfied, because it is the hunger of God in you. Thank God today if you are hungry. If you have the spiritual appetite He will fill you with the heavenly food.

We will just glance at Acts 2:2, 4: "And suddenly there came a sound from Heaven as of a rushing, mighty wind, and it filled all the house where they were sitting. And there appeared unto them cloven tongues like as of fire, and it sat upon each of them. And they were all *filled with the Holy Ghost*, and began to speak with other tongues, as the Spirit gave them utterance."

On the day of Pentecost the Holy Ghost came down from Heaven in His unspeakable fullness. He has never departed, and He will not go away from this earth until Christ appears in the heavens for His bride, and when His bride is taken up, the Holy Ghost will go with her. But He is here now, ready and waiting to fill every hungry soul and it may be recorded of you this morning, as it is recorded here of these people, "and they were all filled with the Holy Ghost." The reason why so many people backslide after they are saved is because they do not go on to get filled with the Holy Ghost.

We may have said: "This is my privilege; if I ever come up to that privilege, all right; if I do not, I suppose I will have to be satisfied." But notice that here, in Eph. 5:18, is a *command* of God, and when God commands you can have no choice. He *commands* you to be *filled with the Spirit*, and the obedient heart says: "Yes, Lord, I will obey Thee, and be filled." Just take Him at His word. That is faith; and when we take the filling of the Spirit in that simple act of faith, the Holy Ghost comes in and makes Himself manifest.

Now, here we read in the 19th and 20th verses what kind of a life we live when we are filled with the Spirit; in a few sweet words we get an idea of the Spirit-filled life: "Speaking to yourselves in psalms and hymns and spiritual songs, singing and making melody in your heart to the Lord; giving thanks always for all things unto God and the Father in the name of our Lord Jesus Christ; submitting yourselves one to another in the fear of God." In the first place we do not need social pleasures, because in the Spirit we are speaking to ourselves in psalms and hymns and spiritual songs; the Holy Spirit makes melody in our heart, and we have a singing bird always within. We love to be alone with Jesus; we like well enough to have the company of the Lord's own children, but we hear the sweetest songs when we are all alone with Jesus. The Dove of God sings the sweetest; there might be some notes of discord when with other people, because they are not quite given up, but all alone with God, if our heart is yielded to Him, the notes of the song are perfect and we hear them, and in return our heart makes melody that Jesus loves to hear.

What beautiful words – "making melody to the Lord," singing to Jesus, and He listens to hear that heart, that is tuned by His own crucified hand, make music unto Him. Oh, who can tell what it means to Jesus, the music of our redeemed lives? We think sometimes we are not of much account, we feel like being discouraged for we think we do not help any one. Never mind, if God does not call you to do great things, just make music in your heart to Jesus; He is listening to the melody of your life and it satisfies Him.

And then it is a life full of praise, "giving thanks always for all things," – the good things, and the apparently evil things, and singing your song of praise all the day long. And then it is a life of humility, "submitting one to another." Ah, there are many persons who seem to learn the melody to a degree, and the praise to a degree, but who do not seem altogether to learn how to submit to others. Lord, make us so humble that we would be willing to allow others to walk over us in the dust, if it could serve better Thy purposes. Oh, that our lives may be thus yielded, and He will make the rest all right.

One more text, Roman[s] 15:13: This is a benediction, and most fitting to close this Bible reading with. "Now the God of hope fill you with all joy and peace in believing, that ye may abound in hope, through the power of the Holy Ghost." Well, if you are filled with all joy, and filled with all peace, and you abound in hope, by the power of the Holy

Spirit shall you not have a victorious life? We have been reading some of the most wonderful words and passages in the whole Word of God. May the Holy Spirit interpret them to your souls, make them vital to you and cause you to accept of your privileges in Christ Jesus.[14]

9
Living Waters

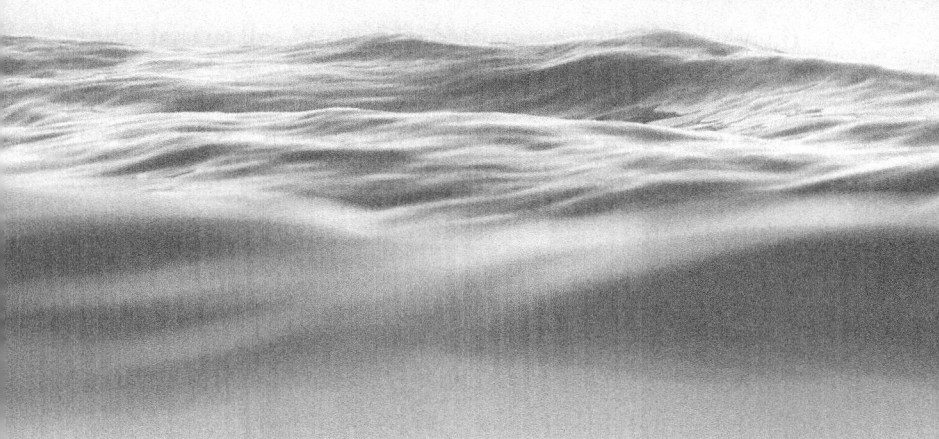

Carrie Judd Montgomery
(August 1896)

*This comes from notes of an address Carrie delivered at the Lytton Springs Camp Meeting in August 1896 and published in *Triumphs of Faith* October 1896.

I believe that there are many in this audience who are hungering and thirsting after righteousness, and this little Bible reading is for them. We will turn first to Isa. 55:1. "Ho every one that thirsteth, come ye to the waters, and he that hath no money, come ye; buy and eat; yea, come, buy wine and milk without money, and without price." How precious is this call of the Holy Spirit to the thirsty ones. This Divine fulness is not for a few chosen ones, but for "every one" that thirsteth. "Come ye;" three times in this one verse we have the sweet word "come." We can hear the voice of Jesus saying, "Come unto Me all ye that labor and are heavy laden and I will give you rest." Come, not to creed or theory, but "unto Me," the living Jesus. The sweet word of invitation is now being sounded forth by the Holy Spirit. You have had a little taste of Jesus' love, but you are not satisfied; you want more and He bids you welcome.

I remember when I was a half-hearted Christian, and it was a miserable experience. At last God made me thirsty for the cool living streams of Lebanon. It is a good thing when we become thirsty, for it is when we are athirst that we are ready to take the drink of cool, refreshing water. It is very sad to find those who are not thirsting for the living God, and who have never had any longing for His fulness. God tells us that we are *"blessed"* when we are hungering and thirsting after righteousness and we shall be filled. Notice again that he who "hath no money" is the one invited. God gives us the living water as a free gift, and we cannot purchase it with our good works, or with our attempts at righteousness. People often say to us, "I am moral and upright and do nothing wrong." That moral man may look very well in his own eyes, and in the eyes of his neighbors, but what does God say? "All our righteousnesses are as filthy rags." In the sight of the great Judge that soul is dressed not only in rags, but *filthy* rags. Make haste, beloved, to get covered with the spotless robe of Christ's righteousness. The "wine" spoken of in this verse is a type, I believe, of the Holy Spirit, and the "milk" is a type of the Word of God, whereby our souls shall be nourished.

Now turn to Isa. 44:3, 4. We often sing about "showers of blessing," and in this verse God promises to pour floods of blessings upon us. He says: "I will pour water upon him that is thirsty, and floods upon the dry ground; I will pour My Spirit upon thy seed, and My blessing upon thine offspring." But notice that it is only upon the *thirsty* ones that God promises to pour the water, and the dry ground that He will pour the floods upon. Dear ones, if you are thirsty today God has this fulness for you. He is willing to give you more than you can possibly think of, or imagine. Let us say, "O God, I will enter into Thy thought for me, for Thy thoughts are as high above mine as the heavens are above the earth." You may not know what you are believing for when you take His thought, but it will surely come. He promises the floods of blessing, and by faith you must take Him at His Word and accept these floods.

Do not wait for feeling; drink the living water and you will taste it afterwards. In this verse God promises also to pour His Spirit upon our seed, and His blessing upon our offspring. We may take this by faith for our children, and again the same thought is expressed in the Book of Acts, "Believe on the Lord Jesus Christ and thou shalt be saved, *and thy house.*" Let us take the comfort of these words, and so commit the unsaved in our families to the Lord that He may work according to our faith and convict them by His Spirit, and bring them into His fold. Cornelius had faith for the whole company assembled in his house, and Paul had faith for all those who sailed with him in the ship. May the Lord give us more faith to appropriate these promises. "They shall spring up as among the grass, as willows by the water-courses." We are to be yielding like the willow. When God sanctifies us by His Spirit He takes all our stubbornness away, and we are like a feather in the wind, or like clay in the hands of the potter. Then we are to be like "willows by the water-courses," always fresh because the roots continually drink up the water, and thus the branches and leaves are always green.

Now let us look at Rev. 21:6. "I will give unto him that is athirst of the fountain of the water of life freely." You have been sighing wearily and wishing you could have the fulness of blessing. Praise God, it is not hard to obtain, for He says, "I will *give.*" It is a free gift, and for whom? Why, for him that is athirst. If you will but come and drink you may have the water of life freely, so that there will be no stint and no lack.

John 4:14. "But whosoever drinketh of the water that I shall give him shall never thirst, but the water that I shall give him shall be in him a well of water springing up into everlasting life." How true it is that if we drink of the world's pleasures we shall thirst again, but the water that Jesus gives springs up within us an artesian well of heavenly grace. Jesus had said to the woman of Samaria, "If thou knewest the gift of God ... thou wouldest have asked of Him and He would have given thee living water." We see the thought again brought out clearly that this living water is a *gift*, and to be had for the asking. The water may be all around us, but if we do not drink of it by an act of faith we cannot be satisfied. "Whosoever" means you, and you may appropriate as much as you will of God's free grace.

In John 7:37, we read that Jesus "stood and cried, saying if any man thirst let him come unto Me and drink," and then we read further that out of these believing ones were to flow "rivers of living water." Then this remarkable verse follows: "But this spake He of the Spirit which they that believe on Him should receive: for the Holy Ghost was not yet given because that Jesus was not yet glorified." Beloved, if you lift up Jesus as King in your heart, and glorify Him, the Holy Spirit shall be given you in such abundant measure that you will not only be satisfied yourself, but you shall be a channel through which the living waters shall flow out to others.

We will close with that precious verse in Rev. 22:17, "And the Spirit and the Bride say come. And let him that heareth, say, Come. And let him that is athirst come. And whosoever will, let him take the water of life freely." We hear again, as we heard at the first of this reading, the blessed word of invitation *Come*, and three times in this one verse it is repeated. The Holy Spirit is saying, Come. His bride, the Church, is saying, Come, and those who hear are bidden to pass on the invitation. The thirsty one may come, and "whosoever will" may "take the water of life freely." Dear ones, Christ's word to you now is *Come*, but if you do not respond to His loving invitation you may hear at last that awful word, Depart. It is possible to be very near the kingdom, and yet not to take that necessary step of faith, and so after all to be lost. Do not wait for feeling, but let him that is athirst come, whether it be saint or sinner or backslider. Come and take the gift of the living water flowing so freely for everyone who will receive it.[15]

10
The Promise of the Father

A Personal Testimony
Carrie Judd Montgomery
(July 1908)

"That we might receive the promise of the Spirit through faith." Gal. 3:14.

"If any man thirst, let him come unto Me and drink. He that believeth on Me, as the Scripture hath said, out of his inner man shall flow rivers of living water. But this spake He of the Spirit, which they that believe on Him should receive." John 7:37-39.

For some time I have been thirsting for the fullness of the Holy Spirit's presence and power. At the time of my miraculous healing, when a young girl, I was first made conscious of the Spirit's work in revealing Jesus in and to me. At this time a power to testify came into my soul, and the Word of God was wonderfully opened to me, so that He has greatly blessed my ministry in the Word since that time. This experience I have always referred to as the baptism of the Holy Ghost until a few months ago, when I began to watch what God was doing in pouring out His Pentecostal fullness upon some of His little ones. At first I was perplexed. I knew my experience, above referred to, was most real and lasting in its effects. How could I cast it away? Then I came to understand that I was not to depreciate His precious work in the past, but to follow on to receive the fullness of the same Spirit.

Before Pentecost Jesus "breathed" on His disciples and saith unto them, "Receive ye the Holy Ghost" (John 20:22). I believe they then received a foretaste, or earnest, of what they afterwards received in fullness at Pentecost. I watched the so-called Pentecostal work carefully and prayerfully. There was much that did not appeal to me. People who claimed to have received the baptism seemed to get in the way of the Spirit. Beginning in the Spirit, they often seemed to fail to walk in the Spirit. They became lifted up, or let self get the ascendency. Many of the manifestations did not seem at all like the work of the calm, majestic Spirit of God. In many meetings there was much confusion, where God tells us He is not the author of confusion, but of peace (1 Cor. 14:33, 40). The people often failed to walk in Scriptural lines in regard to unknown tongues, using them in the general assembly, "the whole church," where there was no interpreter, contrary to the Word of God. See 1 Cor. 14, for careful direction about this matter. In 1 Cor. 12:28, we see that "diversities of tongues" are "set" in the church, and Paul says not to forbid them (1 Cor. 14:39). He also tells us that he who speaks in an unknown tongue, speaketh not unto men, but unto God, and that "in the spirit he speaketh mysteries" (1 Cor. 14:3); also that he "edifieth himself." We are told, however, most plainly, that "greater is he that prophesieth than he that speaketh with tongues, except he interpret, that the church may receive edifying." And yet, in spite of all this, Paul says, "I would that ye all spake with tongues," and he thanks God that he speaks with tongues more than they all. (Why did he thank God for this gift, if it was not truly to be desired?) This chapter is so very clear, we need not refer to it further, but commend it to the careful attention of our readers.

I have stated some of my objections to the so-called Pentecostal work, but God began to work among some of my personal Christian friends, and it compelled my closest attention. One lady I had known for years as a sanctified and anointed teacher of God's Word. She was not satisfied, and pressed on by faith into the fullness of the Holy Ghost. Her experience was most satisfactory, such appreciation of the blood, such power to witness, increased intercessory prayer, such a baptism of divine love. She spoke with tongues, but kept the gift in its proper place. One of the dear Beulah workers also received the fullness, and we could all realize the increased depths of sweetness, humility and power which took possession of her life. Other dear friends, whose lives I had fully known, pressed on by faith and received their baptism.

I began to "thirst" for the fullness. I remembered an experience which I had a few years after my healing, while kneeling with a dear sister, and asking for the Spirit's fullness. He had then come upon me in much greater power than at the time of my healing, and so manifested His sweet presence that it had been almost overpowering. This experience had been so remarkable and so sacred that John 7:37-39 seemed to be verified to me then, only that I stopped short, I believe, of all that He desired to give me at that time, and so the oil was stayed. The effect of this Divine outpouring has always remained to some degree in my life, causing a separatedness unto Him which I did not know before. I had often longed for the sense of His presence to return, as I then experienced it, before I (to some extent) grieved Him by unbelief and failure to go on with Him. Recently I began seeking the fullness of the Holy

Ghost but was kept very busy, and did not actually "tarry" at His feet as I felt I should.

While on an eastern trip this summer, I met other precious friends whose sweet Christian life I had known in the past, but who had pressed on into God's best. I grew still more thirsty for the rivers of living water. I knew I had tiny streams, but not rivers. I tried to go to meetings where people were tarrying for the enduement of power from on High, but seemed again and again providentially hindered from going to them. I then prayed that if it were His will He would let me receive His fullness while waiting upon Him alone, or with some Christian friend. I asked Him also for quiet, sweet manifestations, which would reveal His majesty and dignity, and not such as might seem like excitement of the flesh.

In Cleveland I met a dear young lady whom I had known since she was six years old. Her face was beaming with the calm light and beauty of God's unmistakable seal. Several of her young friends had also received their baptism, but were being kept on quiet, Scriptural lines. I asked them to pray for me, which they did. I said, "By the blood of Jesus my whole being is open to the fullness of God, and by that same precious blood I am closed to any power of the enemy." As these dear ones prayed for me, the Spirit said, "Take." I waited and was afraid to do this, lest I should go back on this position of faith. The Spirit said again, and yet again, "Take," and finally I received the Spirit, by faith, to take complete possession of spirit, soul and body, and testified thus to the dear ones praying for me. I kept on tarrying at His feet for the manifestation of His gracious presence. I asked Him to teach me to "drink." Rom. 8:11 was vividly brought to me, and I saw in a most forcible way that my body, His temple, was to be filled with His resurrection Spirit. That same evening, in a measure, I began to experience His power, but He held me steadily to my position of faith, not letting me get my eyes on manifestations. The next day I returned to Chicago, and as soon as possible made my way to the home of Mrs. Lucy Simmons, of Oak Park, a dear friend of former years, whose Christian life has long been an inspiration to me, and whose recent experience of Pentecostal fullness had greatly impressed me. We tarried together at the Savior's feet. The cry was still in my heart, although I was standing by faith.

On Monday, June 29th, less than a week from the time I first took my stand by faith, the mighty outpouring came upon me. I had said, "I am all under the blood and under the oil." I then began singing a little song, "He gives me joy instead of sorrow," etc. To my surprise, some of the words would stick in my throat, as though the muscles tightened and would not let me utter them. I tried several times with the same result. Mrs. Simmons remarked that she thought the Lord was taking away my English tongue, because He wanted me to speak in some other language. I replied,

"Well, He says in Mark 16:17, 'They shall speak with new tongues,' so I take that, too, by faith." In a few moments I uttered a few scattered words in an unknown tongue and then burst into a language and came pouring out in great fluency and clearness. The brain seemed entirely passive, the words not coming from that source at all, but from an irresistible volume of power within, which seemed to possess my whole being, spirit, soul and body.

For nearly two hours I spoke and sang in unknown tongues (there seemed three or four distinct languages). Some of the tunes were beautiful, and most Oriental. I tried sometimes to say something in English, but the effort caused such distress in my throat and head, I had to stop after a few words and go back to the unknown tongues. I was filled with joy and praise to God with an inward depth of satisfaction in Him which cannot be described. To be thus controlled by the Spirit of God and to feel that He was speaking "heavenly mysteries" through me was most delightful. The rivers of living water flowed through me and divine ecstasy filled my soul. There was no shaking, and no contortions of the body. I felt that I drank and used up the life and power as fast as it was poured in. I became very weak physically under the greatness of the heavenly vision and staggered when I tried to walk across the floor. But when the exhaustion became very great, dear Mrs. Simmons asked the Lord to strengthen me, which He did so sweetly, letting His rest and healing life possess my weary frame. Passages from the Word of God came to me with precious new meanings. Not long after this I had a vision of the work of His Cross as never before.

The blessing and power abides and He prays and praises through me in tongues quite frequently. When His power is heavy upon me, nothing seems to give vent and expression to His fullness like speaking or singing in an unknown tongue. I pray that I may be kept as clay in His hands; that I may be kept very low at His feet, and never get in His blessed way. He keeps me continually standing by faith in His finished work, not walking by sight, and this is my answer to those who might accuse me of depending upon manifestations in my Christian life. He says, "Ye shall be witnesses unto me." Pray that I may be a faithful witness to His glory.

Reports of Pentecostal blessing are coming from all over the world. It certainly seems that it is the time of the "latter rain" *mentioned* in Zech. 10:1.

If so, let the dear sanctified children of God heed the words, "Ask ye of the Lord rain in the time of the latter rain; so the Lord shall make bright clouds, and give them showers of rain."[16]

11
The Life on Wings: The Possibilities of Pentecost

Carrie Judd Montgomery
(1910)

*The following is a sermon Carrie gave at the Stone Church in Chicago in 1910 entitled "Life on Wings: The Possibilities of Pentecost." It was eventually published in *Triumphs of Faith* in August 1912. In it Carrie shares faith-building stories about her own healing and her own Spirit baptism experience. This is one of my all-time favorite teachings, so much so that I used a portion of its title as part of the title of my published Ph.D. thesis, *Life on Wings: The Forgotten Life and Theology of Carrie Judd Montgomery*.[17]

I want to talk to you about "The Life on Wings." Read with me Deuteronomy 32:9-14. That the Lord's people are the Lord's portion is a precious thought, for He left everything in order that He might have this portion. So, I believe the Lord means for us to realize how very, very precious we are to Him. We remember how in our own experience He found us in a "desert land" and in the "waste howling wilderness," and led us about and instructed us and kept us as the apple of His eye.

Then in this scripture there follows the picture of the eagle stirring up her nest. Many of you have probably read the description as has actually been witnessed by some who have climbed to the dizzy height of rocks and watched the mother eagle break up the nest of her young. The time had come when the mother-bird saw that the eaglets must learn to fly, and in order that they might learn to do this, she took her strong beak and made havoc of the nest; pulled it to pieces in order that the eaglets might no longer have a resting place there. Then she throws the young eaglets out of the nest down over the dizzy precipice, and of course, the little things think they will be dashed to pieces on the great rocks beneath, but with one great swoop the mother-bird sweeps down under them, and the little eaglets, instead of falling down to be dashed to pieces on the rocks below, fall upon the safe, strong wings of the mother.

This is the picture that God gives us as the actual way in which He deals with you and me. We can all of us think as we look back, how He stirred up our nests. We had such nice ones; all fixed up for ourselves. They were softly lined, and cozy and warm, and we expected to stay but God came, spoiled all our plans, broke in pieces the nest and tumbled us out. Why? In order that we might learn to fly; in order that we might find the wings which He had already caused to spring forth within our very hearts, but which we had not learned to use, the wings of faith. I look back and remember how He tore my nest to pieces. I had it all arranged. I had my aspirations and ambitions as a young girl. I knew just what I wanted and what would make me happy, and what, in a vague way, I trusted would make me useful, but God permitted the nest to be pulled to pieces.

That awful sickness that followed after I had fallen and injured my spine, those days and nights of suffering, of anguish, of helplessness; those days when the very room had to be darkened on account of the suffering in my head, were but a mere shadow of the darkness that had come into my life and into my very soul. Through this awful trial it seemed as though everything was lost; I could not see that there ever would be any brightness in life. I was a confirmed helpless invalid. For two years and two months I lay there, being taken down at the age of eighteen, at a time when a girl's life usually looks the brightest. Oh, how hard it was! Nobody knows how hard, and I was so hungry after God. My soul was utterly unsatisfied, but God was breaking up the nest of human ambitions, human hopes and aspirations. He knew what He was doing, although I did not.

Job said, "He knoweth the way that I take; when He hath tried me I shall come forth as gold." He knew the way for Job and He knew it for me also. Now, after all the years of blessing that have been mine since I was so wondrously healed by the Lord, I realize more and more it was because the snug nest in which I thought I was so secure, was broken up. Now I am able to encourage other hearts that are going through the shadow and through the valley. So take heart, dear friends; it is better farther on, for as some one has said, there are two openings to the tunnel. We go in at one end, but there is another end to come out. We may be in the tunnel today, beloved, but the other end is there, and you will go through if you go on with God.

What would my life have been without that stirring up? God only knows, but I know it would not have been what it has been. After the long period of suffering and anguish and the coming down to the very jaws of death, the Lord swept His great eagle wings under the poor little frightened eaglet and I found His great wings to rest upon.

He says in Exodus 19:4, "Ye have seen what I did unto the Egyptians, and how I bare you on eagles' wings, and brought you unto Myself." Oh, what a blessed goal! Unto Himself! On the strong eagle wings God bears us unto His very heart of love. Oh what a wonderful day that was when

He answered prayer for me! The time had been set for prayer by that dear colored woman, Mrs. Mix.[18] How wonderful it was that we heard about her at all! The Lord knew what the result would be when He let that little account of her healing of consumption in answer to prayer, be published in a Buffalo paper, and let it catch my father's eye. In those days very little was known, especially in this country, about Divine Healing. Do not think, beloved, we ever had such meetings as these we now enjoy. I would that you might realize your privileges!

When this dear colored sister in Connecticut wrote and said, "The prayer of faith shall save the sick, and the Lord shall raise him up," I didn't know that was in the Bible. She said, "This promise is for you as though you were the only person living." That was a wonderful thought, and the Lord gave me a mighty inspiration of divine faith I never had before. He revealed Himself to me, raised me up, caused all the diseases to depart in one instant of time, and gave me my first introduction to the Holy Spirit. Oh how wonderful it all was! No words can describe it.

Those days were days of praise when it seemed as though I should call upon everything around to help me praise the Lord. I found the eagle's wings. At first it seemed as though I only knew the dove wings; they were not very strong; the little attempted flights of faith in certain directions had to be increased. You remember the Psalmist said,

"Oh that I had wings like a dove, that I might fly away and be at rest." But the dove wings would not take us very far; we need the eagle wings. So through different teachings and especially through many testings and trials of faith, the Lord changed the dove wings into the eagle wings.

But some are saying, "How are we to get this faith?" The only way God can develop our faith is through trial. You ask the Lord to give you a stronger faith, and what does He do? He puts a trial upon the faith you already have. He will take your faith and test it and try it, and you think all is lost, but that very testing and trying of your faith is what brings out the pure gold and causes you to have a stronger faith than ever you had before.

In California we have many gold mines even yet, although they are not so plentiful as they used to be. There are two kinds of mines: one is the placer mine which contains the loose gold mingled with the sand and which therefore can easily be separated; the other is a quartz mine, where the gold is in the rock. When it is free gold it can very easily be separated from the rock, but in many of the mines there is what the miners call rebellious ore; they also call it refractory ore, and when I first heard my husband call the ore rebellious and say it was a technical term they used, I said, "That is just like some people, rebellious ore, refractory ore; the gold is there but very hard to get out." This gold is so united with baser metals that they must have a different process to get the gold free from the baser ore; they do not care anything about the baser ores, they can be burned up or volatilized, but the miners are after the gold.

Now God is after the gold in us. "I counsel thee to buy of Me gold tried in the fire, that thou mayst be rich." They have different processes now, but one process which is used a good deal is a row of furnaces through which it is put one after the other and each one is hotter than the preceding. We ask to be delivered from one of God's furnaces and we may get into a hotter one. I visited a mine and I saw the whole process. First, they broke the rock in pieces and then pulverized it, then there were large canvas sheets spread out, slightly on an incline, and the pulverized rock and ore was put on there and a stream of water was run over it, and some one stood at the top and swept it down carefully. The pulverized rock which was light went off with the water, but the metal, which was heavier, stayed on the canvas and it was swept off in little piles. It didn't look at all like gold, and you know, beloved, it is only God that can see the gold in us sometimes; I am sorry we haven't more spiritual perception to enable us to see the gold in each other. May God help us to see the gold in each other's souls!

Those sulphurets, as they call them, look something like mortar; you couldn't see any gold at all, but it was there. We went into the furnace room, and saw where they were putting it into one furnace after another; my husband is a mining man and he took me to visit this large mine that I might see all the processes.

The superintendent stood by me and we saw a lot of little sparks flying in every direction, and he explained that that was the baser metals being burned or volatilized, and then, not knowing he was uttering a great spiritual truth, he said, "When the sparks stop flying we take it out of the fire. It is finished." That was so good I looked up at my husband and said: "Why, that is the way it is with us; the Lord takes us out of the furnace when the sparks stop flying, the sparks of doubt, the sparks of fear, the sparks of impatience and of lack of love; when they stop flying then God the Great Refiner knows it is time to take us out of the furnace." Let us ask God to do His work quickly that the sparks may stop flying, but when we do see the sparks flying in ourselves or in each other shall we not be more patient now that we know what the sparks are? that they are only flying because God is working with us or working with some other soul? May God help us to be patient with each other when the sparks fly! Sparks are not always agreeable, especially when they fly upon us, but the Lord can make us patient.

Oh, I often think that if instead of getting impatient with the dear tried ones when perhaps their love fails, or their patience fails, or their faith fails, if we could only stand in love and tenderness and resist the enemy for them, claim the victory of the blood for their poor, tried souls, how much better it would be and how much faster the Lord could work with our own souls. The Lord help us! He is trying to teach us to love one another with a pure heart fervently. I understand "fervently" here, in the Greek, means to be "boiling hot" in our love. You never can have the love that keeps up to the boiling heat all the time unless you first have a pure heart. "Love one another with a pure heart fervently."

We want to look again at the thought of the winged life. We get it in that well-known passage in Isa. 40:28-31. "He giveth power to the faint; and to them that have no might He increaseth strength." I wonder if there are any faint ones here tonight. He says He will give you power. The fainting are the very ones to whom He promises power, but to them that have no might at all He increaseth strength.

All that we have must be surrendered to Him to use as He wills. The one thing I found hardest to consecrate to the Lord when I was a girl and He was seeking to lead me to Himself, was a little talent I was born with, and that was a little gift of writing verses and also prose and when the Lord sought to lead me to Himself during that awful suffering, I gave God all but that one thing, and about that I said, "No, it is good and I do not have to give it up." He pressed it upon me that I had to surrender it to Him, and finally I told Him I would hold on to it as tightly as

I could and that He would have to pull it away from me. That wasn't very pleasant for the Lord, nor for me, but He was faithful; He saw I had to take the hard way. So when I got to the place of full surrender, just before I was healed, I said, "Lord, I am willing to have Thee make me willing," and He took me at that. When I got there I gave it all up to Him as best I could, and I never expected Him to let me write another thing.

I had written from a child and had a volume of poems printed, written before I had finished my eighteenth year, but I never expected to be able to write again, and so after my healing it was a wonderful joy to find that that which had gone to Calvary with Him was given back in resurrection power. There only was this difference: Instead of using it myself, the Holy Spirit uses it. God seems to keep it, as it were, locked up in a cupboard, and whenever He wants me to use it for Him, He enables me to use it in the power of His endless life, and then takes it back again for safe keeping. That is why the Lord is pleased to use the little book, "The Prayer of Faith," so greatly, because He wrote it through me. This is a little illustration to show you that everything you have, has got to go down into death, all your natural ability, all your natural talent, all your natural knowledge and wisdom. Everything! If He chooses to give you back anything in resurrection life, all right, and if He doesn't it is better not to get it back. It is an empty life, wherein you feel absolutely nothing; perfect weakness, emptied out for Jesus; you feel nothing but blankness and God causes you to stand before Him. It is just a question of trusting Him; letting Him take possession of your mind, and "when our weakness leans upon His might, then all is right."

People know very little about the mind being cleansed by the blood and being emptied of all its human thoughts. I cannot begin to tell you what God has done in my mind since I have had this fuller baptism of the Holy Ghost. He shows me that people are having their minds corrupted from the simplicity that is in Christ Jesus. He shows me that the weapons of our warfare are not carnal, but mighty through God to the pulling down of strongholds; casting down imaginations and every high thing that exalteth itself against the knowledge of God. He shows me I cannot reason in the old way. Oh the wonderful realization that God has emptied my own mind out, and that I have the mind of Christ. This is so restful; it feels as though my brain was having a holiday, and all the busy, wearisome thoughts are gone.

This is a part of the life on wings. In all the many years of blessedness before this fuller baptism, I did not know what I am talking about now, this freedom of the mind from all care; of course, I had a great deal of blessing and a great deal of freedom from care, and felt that God had guided me and blessed me wonderfully, but I didn't know what I am talking about now. Now I feel that the Holy Spirit holds my brain just as He does the rest of my being, but it is just as loving and tender as it is strong.

Now He tells us He exchanges our strength. We shall mount up with wings as eagles, and this is wonderfully true not only in the spiritual and the mental, but true in the physical, and since this mighty baptism in the Holy Ghost which I received over two years ago, I know what that mounting up with wings is in my physical being. I feel oftentimes when I walk along the streets as though I could hardly walk properly, I am so full of something which seems as though it was lifting me up on wings; wings on my feet, wings on my limbs, wings all over. I realize it as I run up and down the stairs. It is Romans 8:11, "But if the Spirit of Him that raised up Jesus from the dead dwell in you, He that raised up Christ from the dead shall also quicken your mortal bodies by His Spirit that dwelleth in you."

Early this morning as the power of God was upon me, and I was recognizing, as I so often love to do, the presence of the indwelling Comforter, and worshipping Him in His temple, with the Father and the Son, was led out in prayer for different things, but all at once He said to me, "I want you to recognize definitely that I am filling the temple." Of course, I know He always fills it, but this was something a little different and He wanted the recognition that every part of spirit, soul and body was pervaded with His presence, and that meant, as He revealed to me His meaning, that I should drop even prayer for the time and be occupied with the presence of His glory, and I said, "Oh, God, the Holy Ghost, Thou art filling Thy temple," and immediately, just as though a little vial of attar of roses had been broken in this room and every part of it would soon be filled with the perfume, so the presence of His glory, sensibly pervaded every part of my being and even love and prayer were lost in worship. Then I thought of the time in the Old Testament when the temple was so filled with God's glory that the priest could not even stand to minister.

There is, therefore, an experience beyond service and beyond prayer, and that is a revelation of His own personality to such an extent that there is nothing but adoring worship filling our being. Usually it is a blessed experience to be able to speak in tongues, to let the heavenly song flow out, but there are times when even tongues cease, when His presence is so all-pervading and the atmosphere so heavenly that I cannot talk at all in any language, but the power of His blessed Spirit upon me is so marvelous that it seems as though I were almost dwelling in heaven.

I hope this testimony will make some one press on for the fulness. The Word tells us, "That the communication of thy faith may become effectual by the acknowledging of every good thing which is in you in Christ Jesus."

Philemon 6. Through our faithful testimony somebody else's torch may be lighted in the love and providence of God, and suppose we should hesitate for fear of persecution, should stop acknowledging every good thing which is in us in Christ Jesus and somebody's torch should fail to be lit. We have a great responsibility, and if we fail in testimony our own light will grow dim.

If you acknowledge everything that is in you in Christ Jesus He will be ready to give you more good things, and just so far as you have gone on with Him you will be able to help somebody else. I find a great many witnesses who have failed God. It means a great deal to be a witness for God in these deeper and higher things, because doing it means reproach; it means going outside the camp, and I have found some people that do not like reproach and draw back and try to compromise; but I pray that we may always be kept true. Beloved, keep true and testify faithfully to Him. He tells us in Revelation that because we have a little strength and because we have kept His Word and have not denied His Name, He has set before us an open door. I could go back and tell you of one door after another that God opened in my own life. When the little doors were opened He could open larger ones, until now the doors are so large and so many I never know which to enter, only as God makes it clear. So, beloved, be faithful and do not deny His Name.

In Ps. 103:5, we read, "Who satisfieth thy mouth with good things; so that thy youth is renewed like the eagle's." Here is a reference to the eagle again, the youth renewed like the eagle's. Beloved, I do not believe in growing old, do you? I believe God means just what He says. Isn't it beautiful? I never expect to grow old. The years may slip over my head, but what of that? That has nothing to do with it. He who has eternal youth is my youth and my strength.

Now, who is going to trust God for the winged life? You can crawl instead if you wish. God will even bless you if you crawl; He will do the best He can for you, but oh how much better to avail ourselves of our wonderful privileges in Christ and to "mount up with wings as eagles, run and not be weary, walk and not faint." O beloved friends, there is a life on wings. I feel the streams of His life fill me and permeate my mortal frame from my head to my feet, until no words are adequate to describe it. I can only make a few bungling attempts to tell you what it is like and ask the Lord to reveal to you the rest. May He reveal to you your inheritance in Christ Jesus so that you will press on and get all that He has for you.[19]

Part 3
Conversations

Now that you have gotten to know Carrie's heart, I want to introduce you to another spiritual mother who has radically impacted my life.

I will never forget the first time I encountered Heidi Baker. It was one morning in the year 2000 at a chapel service at Vanguard University in Southern California. There, on stage, I saw a little blonde-haired lady kneel and begin to sing a cappella worship over us students. While I had no idea who this woman was, I was immediately drawn to the love of Jesus that emanated from her life in the most powerful way.

At that time, I was a senior about ready to graduate, and recent plans were already set in motion for me to go to Mozambique, Africa, that year with a team from my school. When I later realized that Heidi Baker and Mozambique went together, I was thrilled. Shortly after I graduated, I went to Mozambique for six months. I had the amazing privilege to serve with Heidi right after torrential floods brought destruction to the land, causing many to be displaced from their homes. Not long after this devastation, full-blown revival began to break out. That season of living in revival marked me.

Heidi Baker and her husband, Rolland, founded Iris Ministries (now called Iris Global) in 1980. Their interdenominational ministry seeks to demonstrate the love and power of God, especially among the poor in Mozambique. The Bakers have seen many miracles, and tens of thousands of churches have been planted in Mozambique and in the surrounding nations.

After my time in Mozambique, I returned to California. Years later, I decided to move to England to study revival history. That is where I first discovered Carrie Judd Montgomery. Toward the end of my studies in England, in early 2011, I met up with Heidi at St. Aldates church in Oxford where she had come to minister. In between her speaking schedule, we got together to talk about Carrie's life and what it means to hunger and thirst for more of the Holy Spirit.

In part three, I now get to invite you into the conversation I had with present-day revivalist Heidi Baker, where we talk about Carrie's legacy, writings, and how to stay hungry for God. It was such a gift to bring together two of my spiritual mothers, one who is with us today and one who is now in the cloud of witnesses cheering us on, to dialogue about the fullness of the Holy Spirit.[20]

I believe the following conversation between these two spiritual mothers and me will awaken your hunger for more of God. I pray that the themes the Holy Spirit brings up from our conversation that day in England will help you tap into the fullness of your inheritance in Christ and inspire an insatiable thirst for more of God. The following interview has been adapted for publication. Enjoy the journey.

This picture of Heidi and me was taken the same day I interviewed her in Oxford, England, in February 2011.

12
A Conversation with Heidi Baker

Oxford, England
(February 25, 2011)

Jen: My heart is to see Christians in this next generation live effectively through revivals. I want to see people take hold of all that God wants for them during revival times and also maintain fruit and character after the revival. This passion is what led me to study Carrie Judd Montgomery's ministry. She lived effectively through two major moves of God. This is also why I want to talk with you today because you are living effectively through times of revival and are still burning without burning out.

Many people get blessed during great moves of God but sometimes these don't cultivate sustaining fruit afterwards. They embrace God during a revival season, but then later, their faith in Him fades away. You are still married, you have character, and you live your life with integrity. This is why I want to ask you some questions and gain some understanding about what you've done in your life that can help this next generation to embrace all that God has for them and also to finish well.

Heidi: Okay, let's go!

Jen: I remember a long time ago, you mentioned to me that you love to read the biographies of people who lived in the past. I have also found that there is something important about understanding the people who have come before us. Jeremiah 6:16 talks about the importance of standing at the crossroads and asking for the paths of old so that we can know where the good way is to walk in it. Why do you think that it is important to look into the lives of those who have come before us?

Heidi: It's the power of the testimony. You read about their lives and think, *Wow! Somebody walked that way before, and I can walk that way too.* You gain a greater faith. It's like what happens when you read the Book [the Bible]. You read stories of incredible miracles. Then you see the lives of people in modern day or even hundreds of years ago and all that God has done. Seeing this history helps you to say "yes" to more. I love it! No matter what anyone has seen or experienced, I want more. God's already given us all things, so I want more. Inspiring testimonies spur me on to greater depths of hunger.

Jen: Amazing! I notice over the years that some people in ministry can get sidetracked or fall into sin. In the midst of great moves of God and miracles, how have you been able to maintain your relationship with God and your family? What has helped you stay strong to live effectively for God and also to stay on the good path?

Heidi: Many things have played a part in it, but I think the most important factor has been being "flat out" for God. I've been preaching since I was sixteen when I had a vision. In that vision, I was in a white light, and God drew me up. This was a radical experience with God. I ran after Him, longed for Him, and gave Him everything. In the following years, I had passion, visions, and dreams. I even saw miracles happen. But even with so much of God for so many years, I still didn't understand His Father heart. I didn't really grasp how much Daddy God loves me.

In the late 1990s everything shifted. I was at a revival in Toronto when that revelation of the Father's love came over me. God crashed in on me and spoke to me things that other people might think are ridiculous. Because Rolland and I work with the poor, we were extreme in so many ways.

God the Father broke in on me and I felt Him say, *I'm your Daddy! Eat cheese. Take a hot bath. I care about you as a daughter, as a person.*

Finding out what God thought of me brought such healing to my heart. Then I saw His Father heart for my family. I realized what He thinks of Rolland and our children, Elisha and Crystalyn; that after God, our family comes next. God is all about family. Think about it. God Himself is family: Father, Son, and Holy Spirit.

When this revelation hit me, God shifted so much in me. He showed me that you have to spend time with your family. It's not "either/or," it's "both and more." It's not that you'll have less anointing if you spend time with your kids or if you pay attention to your husband. The Lord's desire is for wholeness and that we model where we're bringing our kids home to.

I want to bring a million children home to our family. But where do I bring them? Do I bring them into dysfunction, or do I bring them into a place of kingdom joy where people actually love each other? This shift in thinking has been a continuing process. It started with the revelation of His Father heart for me and then the revelation of His Father heart for my family.

God is so merciful. Rolland and I have had a blast tag teaming and ministering together. He's filled with the Holy Spirit and going after God. It's so much fun. My kids just love Jesus, and they walk in their anointing. It's about family.

Jen: Yes! And you have your ministry in Africa, and you travel around the world all of the time. When things get crazy, how do you pull away to be with God? How do you make time to stay in that stream?

Heidi: Well, that's one thing that some people don't understand about me. I really love people. I like connecting, and I don't like people to feel disappointed with me. What I've had to do in my life is to make a choice. I make a choice to come away with my Beloved.

I spoke twice yesterday. I barely had three hours to myself, and I had that much time only if I was to arrive very late for a dinner event. I wondered, *What am I going to do?* A lot of people wanted to see me, and I love these people—I really do! But I just long for the Holy Spirit. I want to be fully possessed. I want to be fully filled.

There's no shortcut to being full of Holy Spirit. The only way you get close to Him is to spend time with Him. There's no saying, "I'm just going to have a radical experience and it's going to carry me for a year." No! If you are a friend of Holy Spirit, He wants *time* with you.

Yesterday at Oxford, I made time to be with Holy Spirit. In hour one, I felt Him strongly. In hour two, God's presence felt like waves and waves coming upon me. In hour three, I felt a heavy, weighty glory in my room. It was so heavy that I literally thought I was going to die.

God's power and presence were strong on me. I had to decide what I was going to do. It is terrifying in some ways because it was so powerful. I just said, "More!" I screamed it: "More!" Immediately I felt Him through waves of His presence. I was quite amazed that I didn't die because it was that powerful.

I contend for God's presence. To make time for this, I have to say "no" to doing a lot of other things. I know that sometimes it makes people upset when I cannot be with them, but God means more to me. I love my family and I love our extended family. I love them so much, but He is always first.

Jen: Amen. That reminds me of a story about Carrie Judd Montgomery. When she was in her early twenties, she was hungry for more of God. She was so hungry that when she heard that a friend who lived on the East Coast had experienced God at a deeper level, Carrie traveled to meet with her. When Carrie arrived, her friend offered her some food. Carrie replied, "Oh, I do not want anything to eat; I want God." She then went upstairs to a room set aside for her, and she sought God. I see the same unrelenting hunger in you—you always want more of Him. It's not simply an openness to God, but it's an active pursuit of Him. It's a desperation for

God. I think there is a huge difference between openness and hunger.

Heidi: There is!

Jen: I see that you and Carrie both have a strong hunger for more of Him. Because of that, I want to bring Carrie into the conversation a little more now.

Heidi: I like her!

Jen: Yes! She has impacted my life significantly because she was a woman of great faith. She said "yes" to God all the time. She was healed when she was in her teens. She spent two years in bed, and she should have died. Instead, she prayed the prayer of faith found in James 5, got out of bed, and was miraculously healed. That was in the late 1800s when praying for physical healing wasn't as common as it is today. Many Christians in that day accepted sickness in their lives. Some understood that one way to honor God was by patiently enduring the suffering related to their sickness.

After Carrie was healed, people started coming to her—they knocked on her door and sent her letters asking if she really was healed. In response, she launched a healing ministry, opened one of the first healing homes in Buffalo, New York, and then founded the first-ever healing home on the West Coast in Oakland, California, called the Home of Peace. This was twenty years before John G. Lake's healing rooms.

Heidi: Wow!

Jen: Carrie always said "yes" to God. Not only did she say "yes" to opening the healing homes, but she also said "yes" to writing about healing and launching a significant periodical. Carrie was still in her twenties when she started publishing *Triumphs of Faith*. A minister at her church had advised against launching the periodical, cautioning her that it would fail. Nevertheless, she continued to seek the Lord on the matter and concluded, "I'm going to do it. It's in God's heart."

Saying "yes" to what she believed God had planted in her heart, in 1881, Carrie printed one thousand copies of the first edition, using $50 her brother had given her. Starting with that one small decision to say "yes" to God, her periodical *Triumphs of Faith* was a success and became an important vehicle for spreading fires for revival and healing around the world for many decades. It was amazing.

Heidi: Come on!

Jen: Carrie's legacy inspires me. And, Heidi, your life inspires me too. Because I see so many similarities in you both, specifically in relation to your hunger for God, I thought it would be powerful to create a space for you two to "dialogue."

I will start by reading an excerpt from an article Carrie wrote when she was only twenty-four years old. The article is titled "Ministry," and it appeared in her periodical *Triumphs of Faith* in November 1882. She wrote:

> To obtain great spiritual blessings for ourselves we must pour out our souls for others. There is a form of spiritual selfishness which keeps us so conscious of our own needs that, in seeking spiritual supplies for ourselves, we become almost oblivious of the needs of others, and forget the apostle's injunction, "Let no man seek his own, but every man another's wealth." –(1 Cor. 10:24).
>
> We often feel justified in this selfishness by the argument that we cannot help others without first being filled ourselves. While in one sense this is true, yet as those who walk by faith and not by sight, we must take by faith our position in Christ, claiming that He is to us each moment all we need, for in Him are "hid all the treasures of wisdom and knowledge," and then out of His abundant wealth which we thus claim because He has given *Himself* to us, we must by faith dispense to others. God tells us in His Word that if we draw out our soul to the hungry, and satisfy the afflicted soul, then shall our light rise in obscurity and our darkness be as the noonday. –(Isa. 58:10).

Human wisdom would tell us first to fill ourselves before we try to fill others; *Divine* wisdom takes her stand as *already filled*, by faith in Christ's fullness, and realizes that as she gives to others of this hidden wealth it shall be made manifest. The promise goes on, "And the Lord shall guide thee continually, and satisfy thy soul in drought and make fat thy bones and thou shalt be like a watered garden and like a spring of waters, whose waters fail not."–(Isa. 58:11). Guided, as, by faith in our Guide, we guide others; satisfied, as, by faith, we satisfy the afflicted souls around us; made fat, as we give of Christ's overflowing fullness to those who seem even less needy than ourselves, until at last we are no longer conscious of receiving the former, and latter rains moderately, but our souls become like watered gardens and like springs of never-failing water. *Filled continually*, as by faith we *pour out continually*. Beloved, let us in all our service, in the ministry of prayer as well as in work or exhortation, be like the Son of Man Who came not to be ministered unto, but to minister and to give His life a ransom for many. Then shall we stand with Him, our great High Priest, in our office of royal Priesthood, "consecrated for evermore."[21]

Heidi: I think it's so interesting that I just preached on that! I didn't even know what you were going to read today. It's just so amazing. Carrie is right. We have this inheritance. I keep contending even as I'm sharing around the world and in Mozambique.

I ask people, "Who is going to believe God that you actually have an inheritance?" If you do believe you actually have it, what are you doing with it? If you've been given fullness in Christ, yet there are children dying of starvation, people who have cancer eating their bodies, and people who are being sold into the sex trade as slaves, what are you going to do with your inheritance?

I'm feeling Holy Spirit is crashing in on me like He did with this woman. Just like Carrie. Wow!

I believe we have an inheritance. So, if I have an inheritance, then what is my dream as a daughter? I have a dream to be fully filled. This is the thing: You are fully filled so that you can give. The more you trust God and the more you pour out yourself to others, the more He's going to give to you. That's why I can believe for a million children to be reached. I believe for ships, planes, and boats. I believe that God heals cancer and arthritis. He opens blind eyes and deaf ears. I see Him do it because I'm His daughter.

I long to see an army of lovers, sons, and daughters who say, "I'm a child of God and I also have an inheritance!" There are no lesser sons. There are no lesser daughters.

Everyone can connect with Daddy's heart. Take your inheritance and then run wherever He says run!

It's time for this generation of radical lovers to believe who they are, take hold of their inheritance, and share it with others. No child should die of starvation. Nobody should rot away with cancer. We have an inheritance to share. Nobody should be sold into the sex trade for a piece of bread. We have an inheritance. This means we can make a difference because of the blood of the Lamb and because of the power of Holy Spirit.

I'm getting a revelation. Any dream that you dream is too small! There is always more and more and more. I'm excited! And I agree with Carrie. We are filled continuously, and we continually pour out. There is no need to ever be dry.

He is a living water. I've been experiencing the depths of being continually filled. It doesn't mean I've never gone through dry times, but even in the dry times I just press in. I must have more. When I keep pursuing more of God, this living water starts to rise up inside of me like a bubbling river—and it doesn't stop. I get so excited and when I discover there's more. I just want to shout, "There is more!"

Sometimes I get so happy that I think I agitate people, but I'm not worried because I'm absolutely thrilled about God. I just say, "Holy Spirit, what do You want to do now?"

As the beautiful Body of Christ, we should be like that. There should be no compartmentalization. We should simply say in a famine, "Jesus, what do You want us to do? Holy Spirit, what do You want us to do, as a movement? As a people?" God will say something. He will always tell us what He wants. Then we should respond, "Yes! Let's do that."

It is very liberating because God keeps filling you. The more you pour out, the more He pours in. The more you give, the more He gives.

It is nice being a little older because I can speak as a mama into your generation, and I love it! I do have one big warning for this generation:

> Don't get so busy doing the things of God that you don't spend time in His presence, just receiving from Him. The more He pours into you, the more you will be able to pour out.

Jen: Thank you. Wow, that is so good. In light of these things, what are some of the things that we already have in our inheritance?

Heidi: Healing, food multiplying, great compassion, mercy, kindness, long-suffering, freedom to suffer, freedom to have joy, and housing for every child God brings to us. We have an inheritance for literally anything God puts on our heart.

I'm getting a revelation on this. God keeps speaking to me the words, "In your lifetime." Every island around Cabo Delgado (in Mozambique) will be reached with His love—in my lifetime. No child will have to die of starvation—in my lifetime. There will be a cure for AIDS and malaria—in my lifetime. I believe that if you contend for and receive your inheritance, you can have it. The contending isn't for the inheritance because it's already ours, but it's to connect ourselves with God. We must contend to stay connected to Him.

I notice more and more that there is a big disconnect. This can happen in a marriage, family, church, or society. And it can happen with God. When you disconnect with someone, you are no longer in a relationship with that person. When God shows Himself as Father, Son, and Holy Spirit, He shows Himself connected. Even to Himself He is connected. It's all about connecting.

God is saying, "Sons and daughters, I'm going to connect you with Myself. You can stay connected with Me. You can stay in this place of His presence. You can say 'no' to compartmentalization and 'no' to being a spectator. You can connect yourself with who you are with Me, Christ in you the hope of glory, or you can disconnect."

There is this thing that happens where people start to connect, and then they pull away. I call it "transition." It happens in a lot of ministry meetings. Someone will come up and say, "Okay, now we are doing 'the talk,'" and there's people who just disconnect from being in worship at that point. You don't need to disengage. The talk and the flow of the Holy Spirit go together. You don't disconnect at a coffee shop. As you stay totally focused on Holy Spirit and on what He is doing, then boom! He does something to touch the people behind the coffee shop counter, even to the point where sometimes people start weeping right there because the presence of God is so great.

One time I was in a restaurant, and the Holy Spirit was just falling on people. Then suddenly, two businessmen in suits started weeping. I went to them and said, "What's going on with you?"

One of the men said, "I don't know. I've never experienced this. For no reason I'm just weeping in this restaurant." Their names were James and John. I remember it so clearly. I was able to share the love of Jesus and the power of the Holy Spirit with them, and they both received Jesus as their Savior. The amazing thing is that I hadn't initially said one word to them before they were overcome by the Holy Spirit. They just started weeping because of God's presence.

The presence of God changes everything. The presence we are called to carry—that Carrie called us to carry as well—is not meant to just be in a meeting. We're not meant to live spectator Christianity where we pull God in only whenever and wherever we want to. We cannot say, "Holy Spirit, You are welcome here but not there." We cannot live like that.

I say, "Holy Spirit, You are welcome at all times." I am not afraid to be fully filled in front of anyone at church, at a restaurant, or in a coffee house. I don't care what it looks like. I want to carry the fullness of Christ everywhere I go.

Jen, I want to call your generation to live in this fullness—to stop being spectators, stop compartmentalizing, and to step into your inheritance, your destiny. It is so much fun!

Jen: Yes, we receive it! It's easy to get focused on the doing part and throw out our relationship with God. But walking in relationship and doing the works He has called us to do both go together.

Heidi: Yes, it's not "either/or"; it's "both and more"!

Jen: "And more," yes! It's exceedingly, abundantly above all we could ask or imagine.

Heidi: Yes! And it's much more fun than we thought it would be too.

Jen: Amen!

Heidi: In His presence, you are in this glory realm. If you spend two to three hours in His presence every day, so much more gets accomplished than without being in His presence. People come up with scientific breakthroughs, with ideas in media, the arts, missions, and technology. They discover better ways to reach the unreached people groups by using solar Bibles. When you spend time in the glory realm, something happens to your mind. You start thinking in a different way. You get the mind of Christ and you are full of the Holy Spirit. You need to press in for His presence yourself, but also corporately, and then watch what God will do. That's when the things of God just explode all over the world. It's "both and more."

Jen: Exciting! Now I want to share a prayer by Carrie given over one hundred years ago in 1910 when she was at a church in Chicago and then have you release a blessing over us. Carrie prayed:

> Now, who is going to trust God for the winged life? You can crawl instead if you wish. God will even bless you if you crawl; He will do the best He can for you, but oh how much better to avail ourselves of our wonderful privileges in Christ and to "mount up with wings as eagles, run and not be weary, walk and not faint." O beloved friends, there is a life on wings. I feel the streams of His life fill me and permeate my mortal frame from my head to my feet, until no words are adequate to describe it. I can only make a few bungling attempts to tell you what it is like and ask the Lord to reveal to you the rest. May He reveal to you your inheritance in Christ Jesus so that you will press on and get all that He has for you.[22]

Heidi: Yes, Lord. Take Your people up and in, God. Cause a holy hunger to be fully filled to rise up within Your people. Let them have a holy hunger to say, "Yes, yes, yes! I'm going to soar! I'm going to soar with You. I'm going to soar on the wings of the wind." Holy Spirit, we position ourselves. We position our sails, and we say, "Blow on us, Holy Spirit. Fill us fully, God." Let Your sons and daughters step into their inheritance and believe that a dying world is going to know Your love, God. We pray that none would die without You, that none would die of starvation, God. We ask that none would be pushed away and burned by darkness in the world. God, we say, "Light us ablaze, Lord. Burn in us. Fire of God, burn in us. Love of God, burn in us. Set us ablaze to soar with You in the heavenly realms of glory." Remove every bit of spectator Christianity from our world, oh God, and let Your people fully engage with You, Holy Spirit. We say, "Yes, Lord. Yes, Lord, to the inheritance of healing. Yes, Lord, to food being multiplied. Yes, Lord, to the provision. Yes, Lord, to the radical love, compassion, kindness, mercy, long-suffering, endurance, patience, beauty, and kingdom life. Yes, Lord. We say 'yes.' Undo us again and again and again. Thank You, Jesus!"

Part 4
Spirit Flood

Now that you have gone on a journey into the heart, I also want to invite you into a journey of the mind. We are called to love God with our whole heart, soul, strength, and mind (see Luke 10:27). I believe it is possible to love Him with every part of our being, including our minds. The following is my humble offering to love Him with my whole mind.

Released in 2010 during my Ph.D. studies in England and several months before I interviewed Heidi at Oxford, the following section originated as an academic paper I wrote to present at a Society for Pentecostal Studies conference. When I shared my paper with a few friends in England, they encouraged me to release it more broadly because they believed many people would be baptized in the Holy Spirit as a result. I took their advice and published it as a short book entitled *Spirit Flood: Rebirth of Spirit Baptism for the 21st Century (In Light of the Azusa Street Revival and the Life of Carrie Judd Montgomery)*.

After a short section entitled "Seeds" which was the original introduction used in *Spirit Flood* when it was released in 2010, I then present an adaptation of this academic paper where we will look at the significance that Spirit baptism played in early Pentecostal history at the Azusa Street Revival and how that emphasis may have declined. By looking at Carrie's experience of Spirit baptism, possible ways that Spirit baptism can re-emerge and be translated into the twenty-first century will be presented.

Building upon the journey we have taken together thus far, my prayer is that this conversation about rediscovering what Spirit baptism looks like for today will cause you to cry out for more than just "fillings" of the Spirit. As Carrie once recalled, before her Spirit baptism encounter, she had "tiny streams" but not "rivers of living water." The time of breaking the dam has now come. Even if you have already once experienced the flooding of the Spirit in the past, the rivers of living water are freely available today in new measures to all who ask.

Many have been touched, impacted, and even experienced a fresh baptism of the Holy Spirit as the result of reading *Spirit Flood*. I pray that you, too, will be undone and led to even greater depths of the waters of the Holy Spirit. As you dive in, may the Holy Spirit possess you fully and permeate every cell in your body with His indwelling presence.

This was the original book cover for *Spirit Flood*, published in 2010 while I was still working on my Ph.D. in England.

13

Spirit Flood: Rebirth of Spirit Baptism for the 21st Century

(In Light of the Azusa Street Revival and the Life of Carrie Judd Montgomery)
Jennifer A. Miskov
*This section was originally written and released in England in 2010.

Seeds

Since being in England and studying revivals, the theme of Spirit baptism has emerged in my studies as I have looked at the work of the Holy Spirit in the early 1900s. This has led to my personal reflection on the subject. I was fascinated with this somewhat new theme for me, which was central to the early global Pentecostal revivals of the 1900s. I had already had a deep experience in the Spirit as a teenager where I also spoke in tongues, but this whole language of being baptized and flooded in the Spirit was a newer concept for me.

I became fascinated with Spirit baptism and how it played a crucial role in a great revival. I started pressing in to find out more about it through my academic studies and my devotional times. During the time of my increasing hunger for more of the Spirit, I attended a church service here in England where the guest speaker talked about Spirit baptism. I was marked by the Spirit that night, laid out on the floor, and wanted more. I got home and was still on cloud nine after a deep experience with the Spirit. Then I looked at my phone before I went to bed and it was exactly 11:16 P.M. I thought it quite interesting that it was also November 16, 2007, which was displayed on my phone as 11/16. With the two 11:16s at the same time, I thought that maybe God wanted to show me something.

I decided to play a little game with God. I thought that I would turn to a book in the Bible and look up an 11:16 verse and maybe He would speak to me. I didn't want to look from book to book because then I thought I would be manipulating things. So, I thought for a moment about which book to pick. Because I had been learning all about the Holy Spirit, I decided to open Acts, which I was also going through at that time. When I turned to Acts 11:16 in honor of 11:16 p.m. on 11/16, I was in awe.

In the midst of my journey to England where this newer theme of Spirit baptism was becoming a significant part of my studies and there was a growing hunger in my heart for more of the Holy Spirit, I read that night in Acts 11:16: "John indeed baptized with water, but you shall be baptized with the Holy Spirit."[23] I literally remember freaking out and saying, "Shut up, God. No way. Shut up!" which was my slang way of saying, "God, You're crazy. This is crazy!"

I absolutely love when God is so incredibly real, specific, and present in our lives! Following that account, the theme of being flooded by the Spirit has continued to grip me. The upcoming essay is an adaptation of an academic paper I gave at the Society for Pentecostal Studies in March 2010 in Minnesota. One of the main characters mentioned will be Carrie Judd Montgomery.

I honestly feel like I have just touched the tip of the iceberg in relation to the theme of Spirit baptism, which I am still attempting to process myself. And while I admit that I am still wrestling with these things, at the same time and without a doubt, I strongly feel there is something powerful when our heart's cry changes from "Lord, fill me" to "Lord, baptize me afresh with Your Spirit." And this I pray, that the Spirit may do just that in our lives today.

Revival of a Forgotten Hero
Rebirth of Spirit Baptism for the 21st Century

This essay will explore the significance of Spirit baptism as a cornerstone in early Pentecostal history and look at how its emphasis has since declined in Pentecostal and Charismatic circles. Based on Carrie Judd Montgomery's Spirit baptism experience, I will present significant aspects or approaches to Spirit baptism that need to be recovered, the potential effects of that readjustment, and look at how Spirit baptism can be translated into the twenty-first century.

Rather than engaging with the theological debates surrounding subsequence, the gift of tongues as initial evidence, the purpose behind Spirit baptism, the different perspectives behind Luke, Paul, or John's interpretation of Spirit baptism, or other controversies, my methodological approach throughout this paper is purely historical. I am not attempting to look at theological themes surrounding Spirit baptism as much as I am taking a snapshot of history and observing the effects and significance that this experience played and can play today.

Let me freely state that I grew up in the Vineyard Movement led by John Wimber (1934–1997), where he did share his thoughts on the baptism of the Holy Spirit from time to time. Because I may have been too young when he was leading the church, I have trouble remembering, outside of recordings and books, the degree to which he spoke on Spirit baptism. And while history shows that Wimber did speak in relation to the subject, after his death and throughout my adult life, I don't recall hearing the phrase "Spirit baptism" much, if at all, from those who came after him.[24] While I do remember there was plenty of prayer for being "filled" with the Holy Spirit and even specific prayer for people to receive the gift of tongues, the *terminology* used at the Azusa Street Revival (1906) was somewhat absent, or remained hidden by God, from what I can remember from my own spiritual formation.

My admitted bias here is that I am seeking to see if there might be something from early Pentecostal experience that needs to be recovered, reintroduced, or reintegrated into broader Pentecostal, Charismatic, and Evangelical circles. Because Spirit baptism can be interpreted in many ways, for the basis of this article, it will take on a similar definition to that which some early Pentecostal pioneers gave it of a distinct experience coming after conversion,[25] usually followed with the gift of tongues (although many early Pentecostals believed in initial evidence, which meant they believed that the gift of tongues was proof one was baptized with the Holy Spirit).[26]

1. Spirit Baptism: Once a Cornerstone

In 1906, G. A. Cook stated in an Azusa Street journal called *The Apostolic Faith*, "To endeavor to help those who are sending in letters of inquiry to the Apostolic Faith office, asking how they may receive the Holy Ghost, the writer will state a little of his personal experience in obtaining this pearl of great price, the baptism with the Holy Ghost..."[27] In early American Pentecostalism, Spirit baptism was exactly that: the pearl of great price. Leading global Pentecostalism historian, Allan Anderson, recalls that in relation to Pentecostal fires spreading in the early 1900s, there was an emphasis of "mission flowing from the baptism in the Spirit."[28] The hype surrounding a deeper hunger for and a waiting for the baptism of the Holy Spirit played a significant role in global revivals. Most scholars would agree that Spirit baptism was a major thrust in mission in early Pentecostal history.

In reflecting on today's world, I wonder when the last time in a Pentecostal or Charismatic circle there has been a sermon about being baptized in the Holy Spirit or an invitation for that to happen.[29] When was the last time any of us attended a service and heard an altar call for those who wanted to receive their "personal Pentecost"? And regardless of my own stance in relation to the gift of tongues as initial evidence or not,[30] where are tongues today? They were everywhere at the Azusa Street Revival.[31]

A study done in 2006, which included ten nations, showed that 49 percent of Pentecostals and 32 percent of Charismatics surveyed said they never speak in tongues.[32] For those Pentecostals who still stand strong in believing that tongues are the only sign of initial evidence for true

Spirit baptism,[33] does that mean for them that almost half of Pentecostals surveyed have yet to receive their Spirit baptism? And if baptism of the Holy Spirit was central to a worldwide revival,[34] why is that something that many American Pentecostal and Charismatic churches do not put as much emphasis on today? If many people believe that the Azusa Street Revival was a critical launching pad for the Pentecostal movement in America, which is still affecting millions even to this day, I find it interesting that many are failing to integrate it into their own practical theology.[35] I agree with theologian Frank D. Macchia when he says that he has "thus come to wonder if the relative neglect of the doctrine of Spirit baptism among Pentecostal theologians might not need to be reconsidered."[36]

It appears that what was once a significant part of a breakthrough generation has now faded in many Pentecostal and Charismatic churches.[37] Pentecostal theologian Stanley M. Horton notices that after a revival broke out at Nyack College in New York in the early 1900s and they decided that tongues was not initial evidence, the people there stopped praying for the baptism of the Spirit. He goes on to say that he hopes "that will not happen in America as a whole in the present century. If it does, missionaries from other parts of the world will be coming here to spread the truth and call for a new Pentecostal revival."[38] This is just one account where theological differences in relation to Spirit baptism may have caused decline in it being emphasized further. Additionally, in relation to the Azusa Street Revival, other possible reasons for decline may have been division from within,[39] a lack of love at times,[40] and disillusionment in relation to the gift of tongues.[41]

One must wonder what things in relation to Spirit baptism might be missing since its emphasis has been toned down. Yes, more training, equipping, and discipling is needed to channel these spontaneous moves of the Holy Spirit, but have Pentecostals and Charismatics, possibly because of overemphasis or past mistakes, lost their formative vision to seek Pentecost today? And if that is the case, what might they be missing out on? Or does it look different now that we are in the twenty-first century?

Even Third Wavers and others influenced by the Pentecostal movement might do well to rethink the importance of Spirit baptism to see if there are places today where it has been left out, to the detriment and less effectiveness of the churchgoer or the minister. It might be important to ask if being baptized in the Holy Spirit is a prerequisite for successful ministry and anointing, for cleansing and empowerment. Alternatively, if one is already successful in ministry, will this baptism add anything to them or their ministry or not? A look at the baptism of the Holy Spirit in the life of Carrie Judd Montgomery will be helpful in finding some possible answers.

2. Carrie Judd Montgomery's Spirit Baptism Experience as a Model

The most influential woman in the Divine Healing Movement in America, Carrie Judd Montgomery (1858–1946) had already experienced the Spirit in a profound way previous to her own Spirit baptism experience. As a young woman, she experienced a miraculous healing, which empowered her for lifelong ministry. Before the heightened Holy Spirit stirrings in the early 1900s, she originally thought that her first healing experience with the Spirit on February 26, 1879, was her Spirit baptism. From that point on in her life, she had a very influential and forerunning healing ministry.

Carrie was in her late forties when the turn of the century came with the Azusa Street Revival in Los Angeles in all its glory, making headlines. Though she walked cautiously at first toward what was happening at the beginnings of American Pentecostalism, she nevertheless searched out this "Pentecostal baptism" for herself. Even with her already profound healing ministry and achievements, she admitted that she "grew still more thirsty for the rivers of living water." She said she knew she "had tiny streams, but not rivers."[42]

She proceeded to prayerfully seek God for the Spirit baptism experience that was popular at the turn of the century. She was also encouraged by her friend Lucy Simmons who had already experienced Spirit baptism herself. It was with that same friend, on Monday, June 29, 1908, that Carrie, at fifty years old, prayed for and received her "true" baptism of the Holy Spirit.[43] Immediately following this overwhelming experience with the Spirit, Carrie spoke in tongues for nearly two hours.[44] Less than two months after the event, she recorded her account:

> For some time I have been thirsting for the fullness of the Holy Spirit's presence and power. At the time of my miraculous healing, when a young girl, I was first made conscious of the Holy Spirit's work in revealing Jesus in and to me. At this time a power to testify came into my soul, and the Word of God was wonderfully opened to me, so that He has greatly blessed my ministry in the Word since that time. This experience I have always referred to as the baptism of the Holy Ghost until a few months ago, when I began to watch what God was doing in pouring out His Pentecostal fullness upon some of His little ones. At first I was perplexed. I knew my experience, above referred to, was most real and lasting in its effects. How could I cast it away? Then I came

to understand that I was not to depreciate His precious work in the past, but to follow on to receive the fullness of the same Spirit.[45]

Did Carrie get baptized twice in the Holy Spirit? Was her first healing experience just a "filling" of the Spirit? Was the second experience a deeper expression and maybe even a renewal of her first experience but with a different outcome? Even though she had already experienced the Holy Spirit's presence in her earlier healing encounter, she felt that there was still something more. Referring to the earlier quote, she experienced "tiny streams" but not yet "rivers." When some of her friends received their Pentecost experience and she noticed the transformations that took place in their lives, she began to hunger for something she never realized existed before.

Let's look at the mile run to get a better idea of her situation. Before 1954, nobody really thought that the mile run record could be broken in less than four minutes. No one even tried because that is where the bar had always been raised. It wasn't until Roger Bannister from England broke the record on May 16, 1954, that people began to realize that it was even possible. He ran the mile in 3 minutes and 59.4 seconds. Less than two months later, John Landy from Australia broke Bannister's record for the mile run in 3 minutes and 57.9 seconds. Even today, sports experts regard Bannister's achievement as one of the greatest athletic successes of all time. He broke a barrier that people didn't even think to break before. No one thought it was possible.[46]

It seems in the revivals of the early twentieth century, especially in the Azusa Street Revival, that the Holy Spirit broke down barriers, even racial ones, to bring in a new outpouring of the Spirit that not many had been accustomed to before. While there were stories of Spirit baptisms with speaking in tongues scattered throughout history, Carrie most likely did not come across anyone who had received the baptism of the Holy Spirit with the gift of tongues until just before her own Spirit baptism experience. When Carrie saw deeper expressions of the Holy Spirit in others for the first time, she was awakened to hunger for something she never realized was possible before then. Simmons was one of the first people Carrie observed firsthand who broke the figurative "four minute mile" record or, in reality, had her Spirit baptism experience. Carrie admitted that she was at first somewhat skeptical of the "Pentecostal fullness," but after seeing the positive effects it had on her friend, Carrie was struck to the core—enough to welcome the experience in her own life.[47]

If Carrie, who was already thriving in her ministry, previously believed that she had already been baptized in the Holy Spirit, one must wonder what effect her "second" baptism of the Holy Spirit, with the gift of tongues following, had on her life and her ministry. After this "second"

Spirit baptism, Carrie claimed to have experienced a greater increase of joy, love, power for service, "teachableness," love of the Word of God, and "fellowship in prayer and praise."[48] She described in a sermon a few years after, that her "fuller baptism" experience resulted in "freedom of the mind from all care," which she had previously yet to settle.[49] She also described her life following her Spirit baptism as one where she mounted up with wings and gained physical strength in her body.

Her baptism of the Holy Spirit also affected her ministry. Shortly after her experience, in her *Triumphs of Faith*, she became an advocate for Spirit baptism while continuing to maintain a balanced view that love was the best result of Spirit baptism.[50] Additionally, instead of just collecting money for foreign missions, she went on an international ministry trip. It was during the trip that she was first used as a bridge between Evangelicals and Pentecostals to introduce this new experience and bring clarity and understanding to missionaries on the field. While it is highly probable that Carrie still would have been effective in ministry if she continued without her Spirit baptism, she claimed that the experience added new dimensions to her ministry.

If Carrie, an already successful and effective leader in the Divine Healing Movement, and she being only one of many in a similar situation, saw significance in this experience, then what does that say for successful ministers who have hesitated to explore Spirit baptism? What about Christians who believe this Spirit baptism experience is not for them because it's too "Pentecostal"? Are they missing out on anything? Carrie would most likely say "yes" to that question. While from her example, Spirit baptism might not transform one's whole ministry, Carrie did claim that it enhanced her ministry in new ways and added a greater depth to her spirituality. It also empowered her for global missions in a new way.

Whether it be Spirit baptism or a new move of God, Carrie's approach provides an important example for people from Charismatic, Pentecostal, Evangelical, and even other traditions to follow. She remained open to and hungry for all that the Spirit had to offer, even if it was not what she was used to. She believed that just because some people were fanatics in relation to this experience, it did not mean it was not from God or did not have value. She approached Spirit baptism with a discerning view, making sure not to throw out the "baby with the bathwater." She was both open and hungry to partake of all that God had for her regardless of what it might cost her.

Present-day Christians can follow her path to do the same thing today regarding new moves of the Spirit. The next time a strange phenomenon in relation to the work of the Spirit breaks out, hopefully people will be encouraged through Carrie's example not to miss out on all that the Spirit might have for them just because it comes in a seemingly "strange" package. Nestled in with all that dirty bathwater, there might just be a precious baby who is waiting to be seen and embraced. Regardless of how successful someone in ministry already is, by learning from some early Pentecostals, specifically Carrie Judd Montgomery, there's a flooding and overwhelming experience of the Holy Spirit available for all who want to take hold of it.

3. Spirit Baptisms into the Twenty-first Century

We have briefly looked at the historical importance that Spirit baptism played in the Pentecostal revivals of the early 1900s, noticed how its emphasis declined through the years, and examined the significance of Carrie Judd Montgomery's Spirit baptism experience. It has been shown that Spirit baptism was a focus, a cornerstone, an experience at the heart of a worldwide revival. Now we will move on to discover the significance of the Pentecostal Spirit baptism for the twenty-first century and explore what it might look like when this theme is rediscovered inside, and even outside, Pentecostal circles today.[51]

Spirit baptism terminology in Pentecostal traditions is generally connected to one distinct experience.[52] I wonder what would happen if the metaphor and imagery linked to Spirit baptism was adapted to more than just that initial experience. What if the motivation and the terminology surrounding this theme got applied after the initial experience as well? Once someone has received their distinct Pentecostal experience, it might be easy to settle, check that off the list, and then simply ask for more "fillings" of the Spirit after that.

I'm not saying that Spirit baptism experiences are invalid in any way. I am also not saying that we should seek multiple Spirit baptisms per se. But I am agreeing with T. L. Cross when he says, "If the Pentecostal reality is for everyone, then our terminology about what it is and how it is received must undergo theological reflection of a nature much more careful than in the past."[53]

What if the Pentecostal Spirit baptism language were transformed and integrated into daily devotions? What if Pentecostals and others made "Lord, baptize me afresh in Your Spirit today" a *regular* prayer even after their initial experience? What if that longing found at the heart of Spirit baptism became a normal part of Pentecostal, Charismatic, and even Evangelical practice and language?

Looking at a pattern in history of God's work through the Pentecostal's Spirit baptism, specifically in Carrie's life, I notice that this theme could be explored more in churches that have hesitated in the past to receive this. Not to exclude those who haven't experienced this Pentecostal Spirit baptism and say that they are lesser, but to create space to invite those who have yet to discover it to do so.

There might be even more that the Spirit wants to pour out in us if we just ask.

John Wimber echoed what was at the heart of Carrie's approach to Spirit baptism. In one of his talks when referring to Spirit baptism, he encouraged the people in his church to explore all the rooms in God's house. Metaphorically speaking, he said that many Christians were "saved" in the bathroom and have spent their whole lives there without exploring the other rooms in God's house. Spirit baptism might simply be one room, salvation another, healing a different room, and so on. He believed that there were many people who, because of ignorance and/or fear, did not realize all that was available to them in the house of God. He challenged them by saying, "Don't spend your whole life in the bathroom. Enter into all that God has for you."[54]

Spirit baptism might just be one of the rooms in God's house that needs further exploration. The interesting thing is, many other traditions have at one time adopted this early Pentecostal theme and integrated it into their practices in years past but have recently forgotten Spirit baptism today. There is a need to go back to one's roots and/or influences to find what was once precious and recover it. Broadly speaking, for Evangelical Christians outside the Pentecostal tradition, rather than throwing Spirit baptism out or toning it down out of fear of overemphasizing one experience, what if in addition to the multiple "fillings" of the Spirit that regularly get stressed, an honest look at the cornerstone of the Pentecostal revival was taken seriously once again?[55] It is clear there was something significant that took place in the early Pentecostal revivals in the 1900s that can be reintegrated into various traditions today for possible similar effects.

Whether there is an agreed-upon definition for Spirit baptism or not, whether it is accompanied always with the gift of tongues or not, at the heart of the early Pentecostal's Spirit baptism was a desire to be completely overwhelmed, submerged, flooded, baptized in the Spirit. Many people wanting that at the same time resulted in, or was the result of, the Spirit stirring up a revival. What if the whole theme and ethos behind Spirit baptism, that draw to be completely flooded in the Spirit—what if that imagery replaced or took a more central role in our hunger for the Spirit today?

Regardless of whether we have already had an intense experience with the Holy Spirit or if we already speak in tongues, what if we prayed more regularly for God to "overflow" and "submerge" us or even to "destroy" or "ruin" us in His Spirit?[56] Rather than desire to receive a "touch" of the Holy Spirit, or to be "filled" a little with the Spirit, why not pray to be overwhelmed, overshadowed as Mary was (Luke 1:35), flooded, baptized again and again in the

Spirit so much that one is swimming in the Spirit? Why not move beyond asking for "tiny streams" and instead ask for "rivers of living water" to overwhelm us?

Lives that are continually submersed in the Spirit are empowered to face the challenges society throws, and they can also liberate others through their overflow. How many times do we or people we know merely ask for drops in our buckets and receive only that, when if we were to thirst for rivers of living water, we would be flooded with the Spirit in that way? If I am to make any difference in this world, even after my initial Spirit baptism experience, I still need more than just a touch of the Spirit or continual fillings. I want my desire to be to swim in the rivers of living water, not just in one great experience but on a regular basis. Think of what transformation might result when the desire found in early Pentecostal prayer circles, marked by an intense hunger to be overwhelmed, to be baptized in the Spirit, becomes a renewed prayer for Christians of different traditions today.

I close with the end of a talk entitled "Life on Wings: The Possibilities of Pentecost" that Carrie Judd Montgomery gave over one hundred years ago in relation to her healing and Spirit baptism experience:

> Now, who is going to trust God for the winged life? You can crawl instead if you wish. God will even bless you if you crawl; He will do the best

He can for you, but oh how much better to avail ourselves of our wonderful privileges in Christ and to "mount up with wings as eagles, run and not be weary, walk and not faint." O beloved friends, there is a life on wings. I feel the streams of His life fill me and permeate my mortal frame from my head to my feet, until no words are adequate to describe it. I can only make a few bungling attempts to tell you what it is like and ask the Lord to reveal to you the rest. May He reveal to you your inheritance in Christ Jesus so that you will press on and get all that He has for you.[57]

I pray that a hunger for more of the Holy Spirit would increase inside of you, that your heart would be wide open to receive all that He has for you today. May the Lord seal what has been highlighted through these words and may they inspire in you an increased and all-consuming thirst to be flooded by the Spirit again and again.

We don't want mere drops, Oh Lord, but send Your rain. Send Your floods of living water to drench us again we pray. Amen, and let it be so.

Conclusion
Deeper Still

Y ou have learned all about Carrie Judd Montgomery's thirst for the fullness of the Holy Spirit. You have even read personal experiences she had with the Holy Spirit. You also were invited into an intimate dialogue with Heidi Baker and me in relation to Carrie's hunger. Lastly, you read an academic approach to embracing a lifestyle of encounter rather than just settling for one baptism of the Holy Spirit experience.

As we close, I hope and pray you have discovered that regardless of any encounters you've had with God up to this point, whether you have been baptized in the Holy Spirit and speak in tongues or not, and regardless of every great spiritual blessing you have had up to this point, there is always more of the Holy Spirit for *all who are thirsty*.

The best way to attempt to describe in human terms what is available to us is to stand before a vast ocean and to realize God is inviting us to go deeper. Too many people have gone only ankle deep or knee deep. Some have even gone all the way under the waters of the Holy Spirit, only to come back up to the surface and stand where their feet can firmly touch the ground (see Ezekiel 47). Going all the way under is only the beginning.

God is inviting us to not just have one profound encounter of being all in—but to dive deeper into the limitless oceans of His presence where our feet can no longer touch the ground and to live in that realm. There are greater depths He wants us to explore. The only way to get there is to completely surrender. He wants us to be so all in that the waters come over our heads, and we have no control but are completely dependent upon Him. He wants to teach us how to breathe under the waters of the Holy Spirit. Everything looks and feels different under those waters. The more we let go of control and fully yield to Him, the further we can go. He wants to possess us with His Holy Spirit. He wants to teach us how to flow in the rivers of living waters. He is calling us to move beyond the deep end, to the place where our trust is without borders, and into the limitless oceans of His presence.[58]

No matter how many encounters you've had up to this point, there is so much more of the Holy Spirit to experience and access. You are here reading the final words of this book because God has been drawing you deeper. It's now time to let go of all previous perceptions of what it needs to look like to be fully filled by Him and to yield, trust Him completely, and invite Him to baptize you afresh with His Spirit, love, and fire. Declare this out loud with me:

> *Lord, I yield to You completely. I relinquish control. No matter what it looks or feels like, I say, "Yes, I am all in." No matter what the cost, I want all that You have for me. I trust You are for me and want the best for me. I surrender all. I want more of You than I have experienced so far. Fill me to overflowing and baptize me afresh with Your Holy Spirit today. Drown me in Your rivers of living water. Teach me how to breathe under the waters of Your Holy Spirit not just in one encounter but as a lifestyle. Permeate and saturate my mind, body, soul, and spirit completely with Your Holy Spirit. Fill my temple with Your overshadowing glory and presence. Leave nothing untouched by Your fire and love. Send the Spirit now still more powerfully, for Jesus Christ's sake.*[59] *Amen and let it be so.*

About
Jen Miskov

Photograph by Jordan Griffith.

Jennifer A. Miskov, Ph.D., moved from California to England in 2007 so she could study revivals. She finished her doctorate at the University of Birmingham in 2011, specifically focusing on the life and theology of Carrie Judd Montgomery and how Carrie's Spirit baptism experience affected her theology and practice of healing. Jen is a revival historian, author, writing coach, and itinerant minister who loves to lead people into life-changing encounters with Jesus and invite them to experience a fresh baptism of the Holy Spirit and fire. She is the founding director of School of Revival, which helps to equip and raise up yielded lovers of Jesus around the world. She used to teach at Vanguard University, The King's University, and Bethel School of Supernatural Ministry before diving full time into leading School of Revival (established in May 2020). She also regularly facilitates Writing in the Glory Workshops online and around the globe to catalyze authors to write their first books. In addition to supporting Bill Johnson in his *Defining Moments* book, she has authored *Fasting for Fire, Walking on Water, Ignite Azusa, Writing in the Glory, Life on Wings, Water to Wine, Spirit Flood,* and *Silver to Gold*. She currently lives in Anaheim, California, and is ordained by Heidi Baker with Iris Global. You can learn more at JenMiskov.com.

About
Heidi Baker

Photograph of Heidi and her friend Tina in Mozambique.
Photograph used by permission of Pascoal Mafuieque.

Heidi Baker's greatest passion is to live in the manifest presence of God and to carry His glory, presence, and love to His body and a lost and dying world. She longs to see others laying their lives down for the sake of the Gospel and coming home to the Father's love. Rolland and Heidi founded Iris Ministries, now Iris Global, in 1980. In 1995, they were called to the poorest country in the world at the time, Mozambique, and faced an extreme test of the Gospel. They began by pouring out their lives among abandoned street children, and as the Holy Spirit moved miraculously in many ways, a revival movement spread to adults, pastors, churches, and then throughout the villages across Mozambique's ten provinces. Heidi is now "Mama Aida" to thousands of people and oversees a broad holistic ministry that includes a university, Bible schools, medical clinics, church-based orphan care, well drilling, food aid, primary and secondary schools, farms, widows' programs, and outreaches involving a network of thousands of churches and prayer houses. She earned her B.A. and M.A. degrees from Southern California College (now Vanguard University) and her Ph.D. from King's College London. Heidi is calling for a passionate tribe of true believers in Jesus who will pour out their lives for love's sake, empowered by the Holy Spirit to bring people of all ages home to the Father's embrace. Learn more at IrisGlobal.org or rollandheidibaker.org/heidi-baker.[60]

About Carrie Judd Montgomery

Photograph used by permission of the Flower Pentecostal Heritage Center.

Carrie Judd Montgomery (1858–1946) was a pioneering healing revivalist who was an important catalyst and shaper of what is now known as the Divine Healing Movement. Through her profound healing ministry, she initiated some of the earliest healing homes in our nation. Following her move to the West Coast, she opened the Home of Peace in Oakland, California, in 1893, which is still there to this day. In 1908, when she was fifty years old, she had her Pentecostal Spirit baptism experience with speaking in tongues. She later became a bridge between

Evangelicalism and Pentecostalism and led many into their Spirit baptism experience as well as helped them to embrace divine healing.

Carrie's articles and books, mostly based on themes of healing, faith, unity in love, and hunger for more of God, are saturated in the Holy Spirit. Learn more at JenMiskov.com/carriejuddmontgomery.

Further Resources

If you would like to learn more about Carrie Judd Montgomery, you can read Jen's adapted Ph.D. thesis: *Life on Wings: The Forgotten Life and Theology of Carrie Judd Montgomery (1858–1946)* (Cleveland, TN: CPT Press, 2012). This is the most extensive research done on her life up to date and focuses even more on her pneumatology (study of the Holy Spirit) and her theology of divine healing. You will get a fuller picture of her story and be inspired by the many testimonies that flow from her life.

Life on Wings: The Forgotten Life and Theology of Carrie Judd Montgomery comes from four years of Ph.D. research on Carrie's life and legacy. Over the years, Christian history has overlooked Carrie Judd Montgomery's significant contribution to both the Divine Healing Movement and Pentecostalism. Carrie's healing account in 1879 and her early literature acted as a "tipping point" within American Evangelicalism to turn Christians from believing that it was good to suffer unto God to believing that God wanted to heal. Her healing homes were also among some of the earliest in the country. These things, in addition to her early contribution to the formation of the doctrine of healing in the atonement, make Carrie one of the most influential people in the American Divine Healing Movement.

In *Life on Wings*, Carrie's theology of healing and of the Holy Spirit is explored along with the following questions: Can one lose their healing? What about divine health? Can anybody pray for the sick?

Carrie's approach to the newer manifestations of the Spirit and her relentless pursuit of the "fullness of the Spirit," however that looked in her generation, can similarly inform present-day approaches to revival. Her faith can inspire Christians from all traditions to dive into the fullness of the Spirit available today. There have already even been many testimonies of God healing people as they read *Life on Wings!*

Other Books by

Jennifer A. Miskov

Fasting for Fire: Igniting Fresh Hunger to Feast Upon God (Shippensburg, PA: Destiny Image, 2021)

Walking on Water: Experiencing a Life of Miracles, Courageous Faith, and Union with God (Bloomington, MN: Chosen, 2017)

Ignite Azusa: Positioning for a New Jesus Revolution with Heidi Baker, Lou Engle, and Bill Johnson (Redding, CA: Silver to Gold, 2016)

Defining Moments by Bill Johnson with Jennifer A. Miskov (New Kensington, PA: Whitaker House, 2016)

Writing in the Glory: Living from Your Heart to Release a Message That Will Impact the World (Redding, CA: Silver to Gold, 2015)

Water to Wine: Experiencing God's Abundance in the Canary Islands (Anaheim, CA: Silver to Gold, 2012)

Silver to Gold: A Journey of Young Revolutionaries (Birmingham, UK: Silver to Gold, 2009)

Heidi Baker

Birthing the Miraculous: The Power of Personal Encounters with God to Change Your Life and the World (Lake Mary, FL: Charisma House, 2014)

Carrie Judd Montgomery

Prayer of Faith (Beulah Mills College, Alameda County, CA: Office of *Triumphs of Faith*, 1880). Also available for free if you do a search online.

"Why settle for silver when you're meant for GOLD?"
SilvertoGold.com

Notes

1. Carrie F. Judd, "Ho, Every One That Thirsteth!," *Triumphs of Faith* 7:5 (May 1887), 117.
2. Carrie Judd Montgomery, "The Remnant of the Oil," *Triumphs of Faith* 31:12 (December 1911), 269-270. The word "other" was removed from the first sentence for flow. The original transcript said: One "other" thought...
3. See John 7:37-38.
4. See Jeremiah 6:16.
5. To read the whole story, see Jennifer A. Miskov, *Walking on Water: Experiencing a Life of Miracles, Courageous Faith, and Union with God* (Bloomington, MN: Chosen, 2017), 133-140.
6. To read the whole story of my Miracle Flight, see Jennifer A. Miskov, *Walking on Water: Experiencing a Life of Miracles, Courageous Faith, and Union with God* (Bloomington, MN: Chosen, 2017), 142-155.
7. This mini-biography is condensed from Jennifer A. Miskov, *Life on Wings: The Forgotten Life and Theology of Carrie Judd Montgomery* (Cleveland, TN: CPT Press, 2012), Jennifer A. Miskov, Carrie Judd Montgomery, "A Passion for Healing and the Fullness of the Spirit," *Heritage Magazine* accessible at https://ifphc.org/Publications/AG-Heritage or file:///Users/JenMiskov/Downloads/2012.pdf, Jennifer A. Miskov, *Spirit Flood: Rebirth of Spirit Baptism for the 21st Century in Light of the Azusa Street Revival and the Life of Carrie Judd Montgomery (Birmingham, UK: Silver to Gold, 2010)*, and a chapter on Carrie Judd Montgomery in *Defining Moments* by Bill Johnson with Jennifer A. Miskov (New Kensington, PA: Whitaker House, 2016), 97-120. See also Carrie F. Judd, *The Prayer of Faith* (Beulah Mills College, Alemeda County,

CA: Office of "Triumphs of Faith", 1880), J. R. Zeigler, "John Graham Lake," in *The New International Dictionary of Pentecostal and Charismatic Movements: Revised and Expanded Version*, ed. Stanley M. Burgess (Grand Rapids: Zondervan, 2002), 828, Daniel E. Albrecht, "The Life and Ministry of Carrie Judd Montgomery" (Master's diss., Western Evangelical Seminary, Portland, Oregon, 1984), Frances E. Willard and Mary A. Livermore, eds., *A Woman of the Century: Fourteen Hundred-Seventy Biographical Sketches Accompanied by Portraits of Leading American Women in All Walks of Life* (Buffalo: Charles Wells Moulton, 1893), 512, Carla C. Waterman, "Montgomery Carrie Judd (1858-1946)," in *Twentieth-Century Dictionary of Christian Biography*, ed. J.D. Douglas (Grand Rapids, MI: Baker Books, 1995), 258, and Diana Chapman, *Searching the Source of the River: Forgotten Women of the Pentecostal Revival in Britain 1907-1914*, (London: Push Publishing, 2007), 66.
8. Jennifer A. Miskov, *Ignite Azusa: Positioning for a New Jesus Revolution* (Redding, CA: Silver to Gold, 2016).
9. Jennifer A. Miskov, "Missing Links: Phoebe Palmer, Carrie Judd Montgomery, and Holiness Roots within Pentecostalism," *PentecoStudies: An Interdisciplinary Journal for Research on the Pentecostal and Charismatic Movements* 10:1 (2011), 8-28.
10. Carrie F. Judd, "Rivers of Living Water," *Triumphs of Faith* 1:4 (April 1881), 57-58.
11. Carrie F. Judd, "Living Water," *Triumphs of Faith* 7:3 (March 1887), 67-68.
12. This excerpt comes directly from Carrie's autobiography, *Under His Wings: The Story of My Life* (Los Angeles: Stationers Corporation, 1936), 96-98 from a chapter entitled "Ocean Depths of Blessing, and Further Service" (96-102) which took place sometime in the 1880s.

13. Carrie Judd Montgomery, "Pentecostal Blessing," *Triumphs of Faith* 15:3 (March 1895), 60-61.
14. Carrie Judd Montgomery, "Filled," *Triumphs of Faith* 15:7 (July 1895), 145-152.
[An address delivered at the Sunday morning service, Home of Peace. Reported by Miss Cecilia Decker.]
15. Carrie Judd Montgomery, "Living Waters," *Triumphs of Faith* 16:10 (October 1896), 217-220.
[Notes of an address delivered at the Lytton Springs Camp Meeting, August, 1896.]
16. Carrie Judd Montgomery, "'The Promise of the Father.' A Personal Testimony," *Triumphs of Faith* 28:7 (July 1908), 145-149.
17. Jennifer A. Miskov, *Life on Wings: The Forgotten Life and Theology of Carrie Judd Montgomery* (Cleveland, TN; CPT Press, 2012).
18. Though this is not appropriate language today, during Carrie's time, this was acceptable language and was not demeaning. Carrie herself got kicked out of churches for ministering to black people. She also regularly welcomed students from all different backgrounds, races, and ethnicities to join her Bible school.
19. Carrie Judd Montgomery, "The Life on Wings: The Possibilities of Pentecost," *Triumphs of Faith* 32:8 (August 1912), 169-177. This article comes from an address delivered at the Stone Church in Chicago in 1910 and revised by the author (Carrie).
20. See Hebrews 12:1-2.
21. Carrie F. Judd, "Ministry," *Triumphs of Faith* 2:11 (November 1882), 173.
22. Carrie Judd Montgomery, "The Life on Wings: The Possibilities of Pentecost," *Triumphs of Faith* 32:8 (August 1912), 169-177.

23. Acts 11:16 in *The Holy Bible: The New King James Version*, (Nashville, TN: Broadman and Holman Publishers), 1988.
24. These are from teachings on the Holy Spirit by John Wimber which were produced from the Anaheim Vineyard and captured on an undated C.D. My estimate is that they were recorded somewhere in the late 1980s, possibly early 1990s. It must also be noted that Wimber admitted that he changed his views in relation to Spirit baptism many times over the years.
25. Frank D.Macchia, *Baptized in the Spirit*, (Grand Rapids, MI: Zondervan, 2006), 78. Additionally, many believed Spirit baptism followed conversion and sanctification.
26. Many early Pentecostals in America believed that the gift of tongues was the initial evidence, or proof that one had truly had their Spirit baptism experience. Many who grew in the Holiness or Divine Healing Movements later adapted this stance to say that tongues was a sign, but if someone didn't speak in tongues it didn't devalue or nullify their experience. When describing different people's views on speaking in tongues, Anderson says that "others like A.B. Simpson, Pandita Ramabai, Carrie Judd Montgomery, William H. Piper and some of the Holiness periodicals accepted that speaking tongues was one of the gifts the Spirit needed in the contemporary church, but that to insist on speaking in tongues as 'necessary evidence' of Spirit baptism was unscriptural." Allan Anderson, *Spreading Fires: The Missionary Nature of Early Pentecostalism* (London: SCM Press, 2007), 53 and taken from *Live Coals* 5:6 (Feb. 13, 1907), 2.
27. G.A. Cook, "Receiving the Holy Ghost," *The Apostolic Faith*, 1:3 (312 Azusa Street, Los Angeles: November, 1906), 2.
28. Allan Anderson, *Spreading Fires: The Missionary Nature of Early Pentecostalism* (London: SCM Press, 2007), 14.

29. There are plenty of churches that still speak along these lines and some that probably even overemphasize Spirit baptism to this day, but from the study that will be presented, there has been an overall decline.
30. 1 Corinthians 13. Tongues as initial evidence that one has been baptized in the Holy Spirit is still a controversial issue in Pentecostalism to this day. Some who first believed in tongues as initial evidence changed their stance to believe that love was the true evidence. According to Robeck, Seymour believed in initial evidence of tongues only if it was accompanied with love in Cecil M. Robeck, Jr., *The Azusa Street Mission and Revival: The Birthplace of the Pentecostal Movement* (Nashville, TN: Thomas Nelson, Inc., 2006), 178. He later changed his view to say that the fruit of the Spirit was the true sign one had been baptized by the Spirit. See Jennifer A. Miskov, *Ignite Azusa: Positioning for a New Jesus Revolution* (Redding, CA: Silver to Gold, 2016).
31. To see a brief overview of some key characteristics of the Azusa Street Revival, see Jennifer A. Miskov, *Ignite Azusa: Positioning for a New Jesus Revolution* (Redding, CA: Silver to Gold, 2016) and also Jennifer A. Miskov, "Coloring Outside the Lines: Pentecostal Parallels with Expressionism. The Work of the Spirit in Place, Time, and Secular Society?", *Journal of Pentecostal Theology* 19 (2010), 93–116.
32. Adelle M. Banks "Poll Says Many Pentecostals Don't Speak in Tongues" October 6, 2006, The Pew Forum on Religion and Public Life, based in Washington D.C., USA. They did a survey of the Pentecostal and Charismatic Movement in 10 nations. The survey Sample size: General public – 739; Pentecostals – 119; Charismatics – 421 at https://religionnews.com/2006/10/06/poll-says-many-pentecostals-dont-speak-in-tongues/ and https://www.christianitytoday.com/ct/2006/octoberweb-only/140

-53.0.html accessed July 2022. It must also be noted that in certain environments, tongues are still prominent according to Donald E. Miller and Tetsunao Yamamori, *Global Pentecostalism: The New Face of Christian Social Engagement.* (Los Angeles: University of California Press, 2007). Their book demonstrates the flexibility of Pentecostalism to easily adapt to its surroundings while at the same time remaining true to its ethos and shows the other side of how in some environments the gift of tongues is still thriving.

33. Many Pentecostals today do though, more than Charismatics, still hold on to tongues as initial evidence of the baptism of the Holy Spirit. Williams, J.R., "Baptism in the Holy Spirit," in Burgess, S., and Van Der Maas, E. (eds.), *The New International Dictionary of Pentecostal and Charismatic Movements; Revised and Expanded Version* (Grand Rapids, MI: Zondervan, 2002), 358.
34. Allan Anderson, *Spreading Fires: The Missionary Nature of Early Pentecostalism* (London: SCM Press, 2007), 53. Anderson shows that there were breakouts of Spirit baptism with people speaking in tongues and having similar manifestations, sometimes even before the happenings at Azusa Street. Though it is a very controversial issue to this day, for reference, I will be referring to the Azusa Street Revival as one of the main beginnings in *American* Pentecostalism, rather than Global Pentecostalism.
35. Frank Bartleman, *Azusa Street: An Eyewitness Account* (Gainesville, Florida: Bridge Logos, 1980), a reprint of Bartleman's 1925 *How "Pentecost" Came to Los Angeles- As It Was in the Beginning*, demonstrates one person's perspective of some of the experiences that took place at Azusa Street.
36. Frank D. Macchia, *Baptized in the Spirit*, (Grand Rapids, MI: Zondervan, 2006), 26.

37. "The Old-Time Pentecost," *The Apostolic Faith*, 1:1 (312 Azusa Street, Los Angeles: September, 1906), 1. Spirit baptism with speaking in tongues has played a major part in the Azusa Street Revival even from the very beginning. See also Robert Mapes Anderson comments on this in his *Vision of the Disinherited: The Making of American Pentecostalism* (New York and Oxford: Oxford University Press, 1979), 4.
38. Stanley M. Horton, "Response by Stanley M. Horton" in *Perspectives on Spirit Baptism: Five Views*, Ed. Chad Owen Brand, (Nashville: Broadman and Holman Publishers), 2004, 174.
39. Charles F. Parham in 1906, Florence L. Crawford in 1908, then William H. Durham in 1911 tried to overpower William J. Seymour in different ways to take a bigger piece of the pie. Then Crawford stole the addresses to Seymour's *The Apostolic Faith* via Clara Lum and branched out on her own, and even later tried to steal the name of the mission. Then, even another white person, Durham, came to Seymour's church by his invitation, and while Seymour was gone, completely undermined him and tried to take over his church. So despite the opposition from outside of the Azusa Street mission, even from within, there was much conflict and heartache. Cecil M. Robeck, Jr., *The Azusa Street Mission and Revival: The Birthplace of the Pentecostal Movement* (Nashville, TN: Thomas Nelson, Inc., 2006), 318 and Allan Anderson, *An Introduction to Pentecostalism: Global Charismatic Christianity* (Cambridge: Cambridge University Press, 2004), 35.
40. Glenn A. Cook, a critic who turned in favor of Seymour said it well: "If God's people would only come together and forget about doctrines and leaders whose vision is blurred by building churches and collecting tithes, having only one objective, and that is to be filled with the fullness of God. Doctrines and teaching have their proper place in the gospel

plan but that overpowering, drawing power of the love of God must come first, and our present lukewarm condition is caused by a lack of this love that 'nothing can offend'," in Cecil M. Robeck Jr., *The Azusa Street Mission and Revival: The Birthplace of the Pentecostal Movement* (Nashville, TN: Thomas Nelson, Inc., 2006), 313.

41. When the gift of tongues came out as other distinct languages, it proved disillusioning for many as they were sent out within days, even hours after their Pentecostal Spirit baptism only to discover in the foreign land that they could not communicate effectively. Allan Anderson, *Spreading Fires: The Missionary Nature of Early Pentecostalism* (London: SCM Press, 2007), 27. See also, Walter J. Hollenweger, 'Rethinking Spirit Baptism: The Natural and the Supernatural' in A. Anderson and W. Hollenweger (eds.) *Pentecostals After a Century: Global Perspectives on a Movement in Transition* (Sheffield, England: Sheffield Academic Press, 1999) and also Walter J. Hollenweger's *Pentecostalism: Origins and Developments Worldwide* (Peabody, MA: Hendrickson Publishers, 1997).

42. Carrie Judd Montgomery, "'The Promise of the Father.' A Personal Testimony," *Triumphs of Faith* 28:7 (July 1908).

43. Daniel E. Albrecht, "Carrie Judd Montgomery: Pioneering Contributor to Three Religious Movements," *Pneuma* 8:2 (Fall 1986), 110.

44. Carrie Judd Montgomery, "A Year with the Comforter," *Triumphs of Faith* 29:7 (July 1909), 145-149. It must be noted that she received prayer for Spirit baptism before this and she experienced an increase in God's presence but without the gift of tongues. She placed the date of her true Spirit baptism alongside the time she also spoke in tongues.

45. Carrie Judd Montgomery, "Miraculously Healed by the Lord Thirty Years Ago," *Triumphs of Faith* 28:7 (July 1908), 145.

46. "Roger Bannister Runs the First Four Minute Mile" in *History* at https://www.history.com/this-day-in-history/first-four-minute-mile accessed June 17, 2022 and "Bannister's Four-Minute Mile Named Greatest Athletic Achievement" by David M. Ewalt with Lacey Rose in *Forbes Magazine* at http://www.forbes.com/2005/11/18/bannister-four-minute-mile_cx_de_lr_1118bannister.html. accessed in 2009.
47. Carrie Judd Montgomery, "'The Promise of the Father.' A Personal Testimony," *Triumphs of Faith* 28:7 (July 1908), 146.
48. Carrie Judd Montgomery, "A Year with the Comforter," *Triumphs of Faith* 29:7 (July 1909), 145-149 and Carrie Judd Montgomery, *Under His Wings: The Story of My Life*, (Los Angeles: Stationers Corporation, 1936), 170.
49. Carrie Judd Montgomery, "The Life on Wings: The Possibilities of Pentecost," *The Latter Rain Evangel* 3:3 (December 1910), 22 and also Carrie Judd Montgomery, "Life on Wings. The Possibilities of Pentecost," *Triumphs of Faith* 32:8 (August 1912).
50. Carrie Judd Montgomery, "Together in Love," *Triumphs of Faith* 28:9 (Sept 1908), "'By this all Men Shall know'," *Triumphs of Faith* 28:11 (Nov 1908).
51. Robert Mapes Anderson, *Vision of the Disinherited: The Making of American Pentecostalism* (New York and Oxford: Oxford University Press, 1979), 6, Frank Bartleman, *Azusa Street: An Eyewitness Account* (Gainesville, Florida: Bridge Logos,1980) which is a reprint of Bartleman's 1925 *How "Pentecost" Came to Los Angeles- As It Was in the Beginning*, Harvey Cox, *Fire from Heaven: The Rise of Pentecostal Spirituality and the Reshaping of Religion in the Twenty-first Century* (London: Cassell, 1996), Cecil M. Robeck, Jr., *The Azusa Street Mission and Revival: The Birthplace of the Pentecostal Movement* (Nashville, TN: Thomas Nelson, Inc.), 2006, and Anderson, Allan, *An Introduction to*

Pentecostalism: Global Charismatic Christianity (Cambridge: Cambridge University Press) all give insights to early American Pentecostalism.

52. Stanley M. Horton, "Spirit Baptism: A Pentecostal Perspective" in *Perspectives on Spirit Baptism: Five Views*, Ed. Chad Owen Brand, (Nashville: Broadman and Holman Publishers, 2004), 56.
53. T.L. Cross, "A Critical Review of Clark Pinnock's Flame of Love," *Journal of Pentecostal Theology* 13 (1998), 23 taken from Norbert Baumert "'Charism' and 'Spirit-Baptism': Presentation of an Analysis" in *Journal of Pentecostal Theology* 2004, 151-152 (147-179).
54. This is from a teaching on the Holy Spirit by John Wimber which was produced from the Anaheim Vineyard and captured on an undated C.D. My estimate is that they were recorded somewhere in the late 1980s, possibly early 1990s.
55. See Larry Hart, "Spirit Baptism: A Dimensional Charismatic Perspective" in *Perspectives on Spirit Baptism: Five Views*, Ed. Chad Owen Brand, (Nashville: Broadman and Holman Publishers, 2004).
56. Baumert states that "the noun 'Spirit-baptism' does not occur in Holy Scripture. The verb form of the phrase *baptizein (en) pneumati*, however, is a metaphor which is not to be understood in terms of 'to baptize', because the Greek verb has in itself different meanings (to submerge, moisten, make wet, shower, pour out on, wash, take a bath; to soak a piece of land, a cloth; to color, to glaze; to afflict, to destroy, to ruin)," in "Norbert Baumert "'Charism' and 'Spirit-Baptism': Presentation of an Analysis" in *Journal of Pentecostal Theology* 2004, 153-154.
57. Carrie Judd Montgomery, "Life on Wings. The Possibilities of Pentecost," *Triumphs of Faith* 32:8 (August 1912), article

was taken from an address she delivered at the Stone Church in Chicago in 1910 and revised by the author.
58. See "Oceans" song for a good idea of this theme. Songwriters: Joel Houston / Matt Crocker / Salomon Lighthelm. Oceans (Where Feet May Fail) lyrics © Capitol Christian Music Group, Capitol CMG Publishing
59. Daniel M. Phillips, *Evan Roberts: The Great Welsh Revivalist and His Work* (originally London: Marshall Brothers, 1906 2nd edition), The Revival Library (www.welshrevival.org), 222-223. Roberts' letter to his friend Sydney Evans on November 11, 1904. The following is a prayer of the Welsh Revival (1904-05), Evan Roberts, would send on ahead of him to have the children pray before he came to do meetings in the land. "1. Send the Spirit now, for Jesus Christ's sake. 2. Send the Spirit now powerfully, for Jesus Christ's sake. 3. Send the Spirit now more powerfully, for Jesus Christ's sake. 4. Send the Spirit now still more powerfully, for Jesus Christ's sake."
60. See also biography at https://rollandheidibaker.org/heidi-baker

Made in the USA
Las Vegas, NV
10 August 2024